Milica Vlac

THE
HEALTHY VEGAN DESSERT COOKBOOK

Delicious Muffins and Biscuits, Easy Cakes and Pies, Irresistible Energy Balls and Bites, Raw Vegan Diet Sweets, Mouthwatering Pudding Recipes, and more

Milica Vladova

"The Healthy Vegan Dessert Cookbook: Delicious Muffins and Biscuits, Easy Cakes and Pies, Irresistible Energy Balls and Bites, Raw Vegan Diet Sweets, Mouthwatering Pudding Recipes, and more"

Copyright © 2018 by Militsa Vladova

All rights reserved.

No part of this book may be reproduced in any form or by any electronic or mechanical means including information storage and retrieval systems, without permission in writing from the author. The only exception is by a reviewer, who may quote short excerpts in a review.

For permission requests, contact the author at www.mindbodyandspiritwellbeing.com.

The author and the publisher are in no way liable for any misuse of the material.

This book is not intended as a substitute for the medical advice of physicians. The reader should regularly consult a physician in matters relating to his/her health and particularly with respect to any symptoms that may require diagnosis or medical attention. The information I share in this book is based on my personal experience, conclusions, observations and studies. I am not a medical professional, nor a health expert. Before implementing any of the information shared in this book, consult with your physician or nutritionist! No information in this book should be used to diagnose, treat, prevent or cure any disease or condition.By reading this book, you acknowledge that you are responsible for your own health decisions. Do not take anything from this book and try it without proper research and medical supervision. The author does not assume any responsibility for any injuries or accidents.

FREE EBOOKS

Strengthen your immunity, detox, energize, heal, and stimulate your metabolism with these magical potent healthy recipes!

Get your FREE copy of
"*10 Powerful Immune Boosting Recipes*"
"*12 Healthy Dessert Recipes*"
"*15 Delicious & Healthy Smoothies*"
"*The Complete Ayurveda Detox*"

Go to ***www.MindBodyAndSpiritWellbeing.com*** and claim your book!

Or simply scan the QR code below:

The Healthy Vegan Cookbook Series is dedicated to you – the reader!

Thank you for inspiring me to always move forward!

Contents

FREE EBOOKS 5

Introduction 15

CAKES, BUNDTS, PIES, AND TARTS 21

    Apple Pie with Corn Meal 23

    Fruit Bundt 24

    Simple Banana Bundt Cake 26

    Banana Bread with Tahini 27

    Sweet Easter Pita Bread 28

    Easy Apple Pie 29

    Apple Semolina Crumble 31

    Gluten-free Apple Strudel 32

    Peach Galette 33

    Raspberry Jelly Cake 35

    Gluten-free Pumpkin Cake 36

    Double Chocolate Cake 38

    Raw Chocolate Cake with Almond Ganache 39

    Raw Chocolate Cake 41

    Simple Raw Cacao Cake 43

    Raw Fruit Cake 44

    Raw Fig Cake 45

    Raw Blueberry Chocolate Cake 47

Simple Raw Blueberry Cake 49

Raw Carrot Cake 50

Raw Pomegranate Cake 51

Raw Coconut Cake I 53

Raw Coconut Cake II (Easy Version) 55

Raw Espresso Cake 56

Raw Raspberry Cake 58

Chocolate Cake with Raspberry Delight 60

Mini Chocolate Fruit Cake 62

Gluten-free Chocolate Cake with Hazelnuts 64

(Almost) Raw Cake for Special Occasions 66

Simple Gluten-free Cake 68

Apple Chocolate Cake 69

No-bake Apple Cake 71

No-bake Almond Cake with Pumpkin Cream 73

Carrot Cake 74

Raw Cheesecake 76

Raw Strawberry Cheesecake 77

Marzipan Mini Cakes 79

No-bake Chestnut Mini Cake 81

Orange Tart 82

Flour-less Fruit Tarts 84

MUFFINS AND BROWNIES ... 85

Chocolate Muffins with Sweet Potato ... 87

No-bake Cocoa Oatmeal Muffins ... 88

No-bake Fig Muffins ... 90

Egg-less Muffins ... 91

Gluten-free Muffins ... 92

Raw Muffins I ... 93

Raw Muffins II ... 94

Apple Brownie ... 95

Flour-less Brownies ... 97

Flour-less Coffee Brownies (Energy Bars) ... 98

Batata Brownies I ... 99

Batata Brownies II ... 100

COOKIES AND BISCUITS ... 101

Simple Biscuits ... 103

Gluten-free Cinnamon Cookies ... 104

Blueberry Cookies ... 105

Pumpkin Cookies Variation I (Gluten-free) ... 107

Pumpkin Cookies Variation II (Flourless) ... 108

Avocado Cookies ... 109

Apricot Cookies ... 110

No-bake Maple Syrup Cookies ... 111

Banana Cookies ... 112

Apple Cookies 114

Pear Cookies 115

Festive Ginger Cookies 117

No-bake Cinnamon Cookies with Blueberry Jam 119

CANDIES, ENERGY BARS AND TRUFFLES 121

Fruit Jelly Candies 123

Hazelnut Candies 124

Raw Energy Candies 125

Metabolism-boosting Chocolate Candies 126

No-bake Cookie Bites 127

Carrot Bites 128

Apricot Truffles 129

Avocado Truffles 130

Cocoa Truffles 131

Protein Truffles 132

Pumpkin Energy Truffles 133

Homemade Raffaello Candies 134

Chestnut Bites 135

Raw Hemp Seed Bites 136

Fat Bombs (Low Carb) 137

Gluten-free Pumpkin Pancakes 138

Energy Bars – 3 Variations 139

Oatmeal Energy Bars 141

PUDDING AND CREAM RECIPES 143

Chocolate Chia Pudding 145

Protein Vanilla Chia Pudding 146

Fruit Pudding 147

Melon&Raspberry Ice Pudding 148

Hazelnut Banana Cream 149

Homemade Hazelnut Spread 150

Very Simple Cacao Cream 151

Chocolate Parfait 152

Mint Ice Cream 153

Chocolate Mousse with Ginger 154

Chocolate Mousse with Aquafaba 155

Homemade Chocolate Cream 156

Pineapple Cream with Muesli 156

Coconut Porridge (Low Carb) 157

Raspberry Panna Cotta 158

Very Simple Citrus Panna Cotta 159

Sweet Rice Semolina Meal 161

Thank you! 163

About the author 164

Introduction

*I*n the book 1 of the healthy vegan cooking series, we have explored some of the most prominent benefits of going vegan.

But everything has two sides, and veganism is no exception.

When we extract a lot of food groups from our menu, there is a high risk of essential nutrients lack!

So, in this chapter, I want to share with you some insights and suggestions how to make your vegan diet healthier, so you can get the most out of this regimen!

If you are currently thinking about going vegan, take a look at the most common mistakes people make:

1. Not taking enough fiber

    Going vegan does not necessarily mean your diet is healthy and nutritious! The chances of leaning towards too much white bread and processed veggies (like potato chips), are quite high. But they are vegan, right? So, what's the problem?

    The issue stems from not taking enough fiber with the food! Although our bodies are not equipped to digest water-insoluble fiber (unlike ruminants), it is still essential for our health and wellbeing. It slows down the absorption of the carbohydrates and prevents form high blood sugar spikes. It also mechanically, but gently at the same time, brushes and stimulates the intestinal walls, preventing and healing from constipation. And last, but not least – fiber is the main food source for the beneficial colon bacteria in our guts. They are responsible for our natural immunity and good digestion! You can learn more about boosting your colon health and natural defense mechanisms in my book "Build Your Immune System Fast"

So, my first health suggestion when going vegan is not to forget about the daily amounts of fiber. Swap white flour with the wholegrain non-GMO types (like spelt, emmer, einkorn, etc.)! Also, add more veggies, leafy greens, seeds, and nuts to your healthy diet as well.

2. Too much white sugar

    The same goes for the desserts as well. When going vegan, there is a high chance of falling for high-calorie and high-sugary foods instead of the healthy sweet stuff. Remember that not everything on the market labeled "vegan" or "organic" is healthy! Lots of companies are trying to cash on the latest vegan and bio trends, offering low quality products which contain artificial sweeteners, white sugar, corn syrup, etc.

    Be extremely careful if you have high blood sugar levels, or insulin resistance, and always read the labels!

    And, of course, it is always a good idea to munch on some fresh fruits, veggies, and homemade fiber desserts instead of the store-bought stuff full of preservatives! In this cookbook, you will find a ton of ideas and recipes with natural ingredients!

    Also, remember to check out my FREE book bundle packed with awesome immune boosting smoothies and healthy dessert recipes (without any white flour, white sugar, or artificial sweeteners)!

You can find them in my blog ***mindbodyandspiritwellbeing.com***

3. Not enough protein

   Yes, we can't discuss the pitfalls of going vegan without mentioning the protein topic!

   But it's true - vegan food can be rather light and delicious, and keeping track of the amino acid consumption can be tricky!

   So, try your best to frequently add protein packed foods like, lentils, beans (especially mung beans – they are less gassy), chickpeas, seeds, and raw nuts. Also, I highly recommend using a calculator to easily check your macronutrients and micronutrients for the day! My favorite one is **Cronometer**, which lets you track everything – your daily calories intake, carbohydrates, proteins, fats, amino acids, vitamins, microelements, minerals, energy spent, your normal metabolism, and much more!

   And, the good news is – it is absolutely FREE to use!

4. Poor teeth health

   Unfortunately, the vegan diet can pose a certain level of risks for the teeth, if not executed correctly. Usually, when we exclude all the animal products from the menu, what's left are fruits and veggies containing plenty of carbohydrates.

   Consuming lots of carbs, even in the form of fruits and legumes, can be harmful for our fangs. Because as we know, carbohydrates are the main culprit for tooth decay!

That is why you need to take extra care and some preventive measures.

Here are some ideas:
- Rinse your mouth after each carb-rich meal – you can use diluted silver water, propolis tincture (also diluted), or simply swish it with some clean water. **Do not brush your teeth for 30 minutes after you have consumed fruits (especially citruses), or something acidic (like apple cider vinegar)!** They soften the enamel and make it more vulnerable - brushing it will harm it even more easily!
- Use oil pulling with coconut oil (or any other type of cold pressed oil) first thing in the morning!
- Eat plenty of foods packed with Calcium (leafy greens, sesame seeds, sweet potatoes, carrots, etc.).
- Increase the Omega-3 and Omega-6 consumption – don't be afraid to take more natural oils from coconuts, avocados, olives, flax seeds, and so on.
- And of course – visit your dentist at least once a year!

These were my suggestions for a healthy vegan diet, even if you follow this diet regimen for a set period of time (for example, during Lent).

It is always a good idea to keep these in mind so that you can benefit fully from this diet plan!

This cookbook is intended to follow these suggestions – it does not include added white sugar, white flour, artificial substances, and preservatives.

Also, keep in mind that if a given recipe seems too "heavy" and packed with more calories, you can always experiment and substitute the ingredients with your preferences.

For example, agave syrup can be swapped with stevia liquid which contains zero calories; wholegrain flour can be changed to their gluten-free and low-carb versions like almond flour or coconut flour.

I think cooking is a personal field of self-expression and experimentation.

So, don't be afraid to tweak the recipes and add something from your unique gifted self!

Feel free to send me your wonderful creations via social media!

You can find me at:
http://mindbodyandspiritwellbeing.com
https://facebook.com/**mindbodyspiritwellbeing**
https://www.pinterest.com/**milicavladova**
https://twitter.com/**Holistic_Milky**
https://www.instagram.com/**milicavladova**
(use the hashtag *#holisticmilky*)
https://www.yummly.com/page/**mindbodyandspiritwellbeing**

I am eagerly looking forward to hearing from you!

Happy cooking!

CAKES, BUNDTS, PIES, AND TARTS

Apple Pie with Corn Meal

Ingredients:

4 cups **Apples** (preferably sour)
1 cup **Corn meal** (non-GMO)
1 cup **Wholegrain flour of choice** (preferably gluten-free)
2 tsps. **Baking powder**
8 Tbsps. **Coconut butter**
1 cup **Coconut sugar** (or other healthy sweetener of choice)
1 tsp. **Cinnamon**
1/2 cup **Walnuts**

Instructions:

Remove the seeds from the apples and grind the fruits in a kitchen chopper. Grind the walnuts as well – you do not need to turn them into powder.

Next, mix the apple puree with the cinnamon and the ground walnuts.

In another bowl, combine the dry ingredients – the corn meal, the flour, baking powder and sugar.

Melt the butter.

Next, take a baking pan (about 8"/8") and cover it with parchment paper.

Take 1/3 of the apple mix and spread it at the bottom of the pan. Cover it with 1/3 of the dry ingredient mix and pour some of the melted butter (about 2-3 Tbsps.).

Continue to interchange the layers until you finish with the last batch of dry flour mix at the top. Remember to pour some melted butter as well.

Heat the oven at 180° C/ 356° F and bake for about 40 minutes until fully cooked.

Leave the pie to cool down and rest overnight.

Fruit Bundt

Ingredients:

For mixture #1:
2 **Bananas**
1/2 cup **Dried plums**
1/2 cup **Water**
1 cup **Olive oil**
1 cup **Maple syrup** (or other sweetener of choice)
5 Tbsps. **Cacao powder**
5 Tbsps. **Ground flax seeds**
1/2 tsp. **Vanilla extract**
1 Tbsp. **Apple cider vinegar**

For mixture #2:
1 cup **Millet flour**
1/2 cup **Rice flour**
1 cup **Buckwheat flour**
1/2 cup **Coconut shreds**
1 tsp. **Baking powder**
1 tsp. **Baking soda**
A pinch of **Salt**

Instructions:

First, we need to prepare the dry plums from the day before.

Pit the fruits, if not done so already, and soak them in some water for 24 hours.

Next, puree the plums with a hand blender without straining them.

Now, we can start with the cake itself!

Cut the banana in medium pieces and blend it with the plums.

Cover the flax seeds with some water and soak them for 10 minutes until they thicken.

Now, start adding each ingredient as they are listed as you stir and blend to form mixture #1.

Next, blend the dry ingredients in another bowl to form mixture #2.

Start combining both mixtures as you gently and carefully stir and homogenize the batter.

Heat the oven to 190° C/ 374° F and bake the dessert until fully cooked (the toothpick comes out clean).

Leave it aside to cool down and remove from the baking mold.

If you wish, you can decorate with whatever you prefer.

Bon appetite!

Simple Banana Bundt Cake

Ingredients:

2-3 **Bananas** (fully ripe and sweet)
1 cup **Coconut sugar** (or maple syrup)
1 cup **Wholegrain flour**
1/2 cup **Olive oil**
1 tsp. **Cinnamon**
1 tsp. **Baking soda**
1 tsp. **Vanilla extract**
1 tsp. **Baking powder**

Instructions:

First, mash the bananas and blend them with the sugar until homogeneous.

You can use a hand mixer to make the process easier.

Next, add the remaining ingredients and blend again nicely.

Start heating the oven to 180° C/ 356° F.

Now, pour the batter into a non-stick bundt cake mold and bake in the hot oven until fully cooked (when the toothpick comes out clean).

If you use a regular baking pan, make sure you grease it with some oil and cover with flour to prevent the cake from sticking to the container.

Banana Bread with Tahini

Ingredients:

2 **Bananas** (fully ripe)
3 Tbsps. **Coconut flour**
1 Tbsp. **Coconut butter**
1 Tbsp. **Sesame tahini** (or hazelnut, almond, etc.)
1 Tbsp. **Vegan chocolate chips**
1 tsp. **Baking powder**

Instructions:

This recipe is unbelievably easy and simple!

You can start by heating the oven to 200° C/ 392° F.

Next, mash the bananas and blend them with the coconut flour, the butter, the tahini, and the baking powder.

Now, add the chocolate chips and stir with a spoon.

Pour the mixture into a baking mold and bake for about 20-30 minutes until fully cooked (when the toothpick comes out clean).

Leave the dessert to cool down completely, and then, you can remove it from the mold and serve!

My notes:

Sweet Easter Pita Bread

Ingredients:

1 cup **All-purpose wholegrain flour**
1/2 cup **Almond milk** (or coconut, rice, soy, etc.)
2 Tbsps. **Muscovado sugar**
2 1/2 Tbsps. **Coconut butter** (melted)
1 tsp. **Dry yeast**
1/2 tsp. **Vanilla extract**
A pinch of **Salt**
3 Tbsps. **Vegan chocolate chips**
3-4 Tbsps. **Raisins**

Instructions:

First, heat the milk until it becomes slightly warm.

Next, mix 3 tablespoons of the flour with the sugar, the vanilla extract, and the yeast.

Pour the milk and blend completely until homogeneous.

Leave the mixture to rise for at least 10 minutes.

Next, place the flour in a large bowl and make a hole at the center.

Pour the yeast mixture in this crater along with the coconut butter, and the salt.

Now, simply stir and knead the dough until fully blended.

Shape it as one large ball and grease it with some more coconut butter.

Leave it to rise for at least an hour in a warm place.

Next, when the mixture doubles it size, knead the dough one more time and mix it with the chocolate chips and the raisins.

Leave it to rise once again for about an hour and a half.

Then, you can start heating the oven to 200° C/ 392° F.

When the dough is ready, transfer it into a flat baking mold and bake for about 30 minutes (until the toothpick comes out clean).

Voila!

Easy Apple Pie

Ingredients:

3 **Apples** (sweet)
1 tsp. **Baking soda**
5 Tbsps. **Maple syrup** (or agave)
7 Tbsps. **Coconut butter**
1 1/2 cup **Wholegrain flour of choice** (preferably gluten-free)
1 cup **Ground walnuts**
1 tsp. **Cinnamon**
A fistful of **Dry plums**

Instructions:

Take 2 of the apples, remove their seeds and grind the fruits (or grate them). Dice the last apple in cubes.

Next, heat the butter until it softens.

Cut the dry plums in small pieces.

Now, we can prepare the batter.

Simply combine all ingredients and stir until they blend completely. You can use a hand mixer, if you wish.

In the meantime, heat the oven at 190° C/ 374° F.

Take a square cake mold and grease it with some coconut butter (or olive oil).

Pour the batter in and bake the pie for about 40 minutes until fully cooked.

Wait for the dessert to cool down completely before cutting it in pieces!

Enjoy!

My notes:

Apple Semolina Crumble

Ingredients:

1 lb. **Apples** (4 cups)
1 cup **Semolina**
1 cup **Spelt flour**
2 tsps. **Baking powder**
1/2 cup **Coconut butter** (melted)
3-4 Tbsps. **Muscovado sugar**
4 Tbsps. **Beet syrup** (or maple syrup)
1 tsp. **Cinnamon**
1/2 cup **Walnuts**

Instructions:

First, remove the seeds from the apples and grate the fruits (or mince them in a kitchen chopper).

Grind the walnuts as well (be careful not to overdo it and turn them into powder).

Next, mix the apple puree with the walnuts, the beet syrup, and the cinnamon.

Combine the dry ingredients in another container – the flour, semolina, baking powder, and the sugar.

Now, take a flat baking pan (or a casserole) and cover it with parchment paper.

Next, pour 1/3 of the apple mixture at the bottom.

Cover with 1/3 of the dry compounds and pour some melted butter on top.

Repeat with the remaining of the ingredients.

Heat the oven to 180° C/ 356° F and bake for about 40 minutes until fully cooked.

Gluten-free Apple Strudel

Ingredients:

2 lbs. **Apples**
1 cup **Walnuts**
4-5 Tbsps. **Coconut flour**
1 tsp. **Cinnamon**
1 tsp. **Baking powder**

Instructions:

First, grind the walnuts until powdered.

Next, cut the apples in quarters and remove the seeds.

Slice a couple of pieces and leave them aside for decoration. Bring the rest of the fruits in the kitchen robot and blend with the walnuts until you have a homogeneous puree.

Next, add the remaining ingredients and blend again. Now, you can start heating the oven to 170° C/338° F (with a fan, if you have that option).

Transfer the dough into a baking mold covered with parchment paper and decorate with the apple slices on top.

Bake in the hot oven for about 80 minutes until fully cooked. Finally, leave the dessert to cool down completely and let it chill in the fridge.

Serve cold.

Find 300+ more gluten-free recipes for the whole family and for all occasions in "The Gluten Free Cookbook Series Bundle"!

Peach Galette

Ingredients:

For the dough:
1 cup **Fine oatmeal**
1/2 cup **Wholegrain flour of choice**
1/2 cup **Coconut butter** (soft)
2 Tbsps. **Coconut sugar**
1 Tbsp. **Poppy seeds**
A pinch of **Salt**
1/4 cup **Water**

For the stuffing:
2 **Peaches**
5-6 **Ground hazelnuts**
1 Tbsp. **Coconut sugar**
1 **Vanilla pod** (or vanilla extract)

Instructions:

First, grind the oatmeal in the kitchen chopper until powdered.

Next, add the remaining dry ingredients – the flour, the coconut sugar, the poppy seeds, and the salt.

Now, add the soft butter and blend completely.

As you continue to blend the compounds, start slowly adding the water (one spoon at a time) until you have nice and soft non-stocky dough.

If you need to, adjust the quantity of the flour or the water to reach that consistency.

Next, form a ball from the dough, wrap it in kitchen foil and place it in the fridge to rest for half an hour.

Meanwhile, cut the peaches in thin slices and cover them with the coconut sugar and the ground vanilla beans.

Stir to evenly distribute the flavors.

Now, take out the dough from the fridge and remove the foil.

Roll it out in a circle on a parchment paper – as thin as possible (around half a centimeter/ 0.2 inch).

Start heating the oven to 180° C/ 356° F.

Next, transfer the pastry with the parchment paper into a baking tray and place the sweet peach slices at the center.

Remember to leave approx. 2 inches around the edge of the dough.

Now, tuck the corners of the galette to wrap the peach filling and then, garnish with the hazelnuts.

Bake the dessert for about 30-35 minutes in the hot oven until fully cooked.

Let it cool down a bit before cutting and serving!

My notes:

Raspberry Jelly Cake

Ingredients:

For the cake base:
1/2 cup **Raw cashew**
1/2 cup **Raw sunflower seeds** (peeled)
2 Tbsps. **Coconut butter** (melted)
2-3 Tbsps. **Flax seed powder**
12-15 **Dates** (pitted)

For the jelly:
2 cups **Raspberries**
1 cup **Water**
1 1/2 Tbsp. **Agar-agar**
Some **Water**
1-2 Tbsps. **Honey** (maple syrup for strict vegans)
Some more **Raspberries** (for decoration)

Instructions:

First, we can prepare the jelly, because it will consume quite some time.

Mix the raspberries with the water in a metal pot and heat them.

Stir well to blend them as much as possible.

In the meantime, mix the agar with some water and stir.

Next, heat it in a double boiler until it melts completely.

Now, mix the agar with the hot raspberries and stir well.

Take the mixture off the heat and let it cool down to body temperature.

Next, add the honey and stir again nicely.

Consecutively, we can start making the cake itself.

Blend all ingredients in a kitchen chopper or a robot until fully homogenous.

Transfer the mixture in an adjustable cake ring mold. Press gently to form the base of the cake.

Next, pour the liquid jelly on top of the base layer.

Garnish with some raspberries, and bring the cake in the fridge for several hours to set.

Gluten-free Pumpkin Cake

Ingredients:

1 cup **Pumpkin**
1 cup **Carrots**
1/2 cup **Rice flour** (or millet)
2 Tbsps. **Carob powder**
5 Tbsps. **Coconut shreds**
2 Tbsps. **Coconut sugar** (or maple syrup)
2 Tbsps. **Sesame seeds**
1/2 tsp. **Cinnamon**
A pinch of **Himalayan salt**

Instructions:

First, grind the pumpkin and the carrots or mince them in a kitchen chopper.

Next, simply add the remaining compounds and blend until homogeneous.

Start heating the oven to 180° C/ 356° F.

Now, pour the batter into a flat baking mold covered with parchment paper.

Bake for about half an hour until fully cooked. The time may vary depending on the size of the pan and the thickness of the cake.

Check with a toothpick to make sure it is ready!

*Find 300+ more gluten-free recipes for the whole family and for all occasions in "The Gluten Free Cookbook Series Bundle"!

My notes:

Double Chocolate Cake

Ingredients:

For the base layer:
1 1/2 cup **Walnuts**
2 Tbsps. **Coconut butter**
2-3 Tbsps. **Maple syrup**
3-4 Tbsps. (heaped) **Cacao powder**
1 tsp. **Vanilla extract**

For the cream:
1 **Banana** (fully ripe)
1 **Avocado** (fully ripe)
2 Tbsps. **Maple syrup**
1/4 cup **Vegan milk of choice**
5-6 Tbsps. **Cacao powder**
1 Tbsp. (heaped) **Sesame tahini**
2 Tbsps. **Coconut butter**
1 tsp. **Rum**

Instructions:

Combine all ingredients for the cake crust in a kitchen chopper or a robot and blend until fully homogeneous. Next, transfer into a cake ring (with approx. 6 inch diameter) and spread the mixture at the bottom of the container.

Then, simply blend all the compounds for the chocolate cream and pour on top of the cake. Level the cream with a knife or a spatula and bring the dessert in the freezer for about half an hour to set. Garnish with whatever you prefer. and release from the mold!

Raw Chocolate Cake with Almond Ganache

Ingredients:

For the base layer:
1/2 cup **Almonds**
2 Tbsps. **Sunflower seeds**
3-4 Tbsps. **Coconut shreds**
A pinch of **Salt**
1 Tbsp. **Cacao powder**
1 tsp. **Cinnamon**
6 **Dates**
1 Tbsp. **Coconut butter**

For the cream:
12 **Dates**
1/2 cup **Cashew**
2 Tbsps. **Lukuma**
4 Tbsps. **Almond tahini**
3-4 Tbsps. **Coconut milk**
1/2 tsp. **Salt**
1 tsp. **Cinnamon**
2 tsps. **Vanilla extract**
3 tsps. **Maple syrup**
4 Tbsps. **Coconut butter**

For the ganache:
2 tsps. **Cocoa butter** (melted)
3 Tbsps. **Almond tahini**
1 1/2 Tbsp. **Cacao powder**
4 Tbsps. **Maple syrup**
A pinch of **Salt**

1 tsp. **Vanilla extract**
3-4 Tbsps. **Coconut milk**

Instructions:

First, soak all the dates and the cashew (separately) overnight and wash them thoroughly the next day. Now, we can proceed to the cake!

Grind the almonds in a kitchen chopper until powdered. Alternatively, you can use ready-made ground almond flour.

Next, add all the remaining ingredients for the base layer (except the dates and the coconut butter) and blend until fully homogeneous.

Now, start adding the dates one by one as you continue to blend the mixture. Finally, add the soft coconut butter and mix again. Transfer the mixture into a flat cake pan (preferably a cake ring) and press to form the base for the cake.

Place the container in the fridge to set a bit until we prepare the rest of the dessert.

Now, we move to the cream. Place the soaked cashew and the dates (pitted) in a kitchen chopper with just a little bit of water (2 tsps.) and blend them completely. Add the remaining ingredients except the coconut butter and continue to homogenize the mixture.

Finally, add the coconut butter and blend the mass one last time. Pour the cream onto the cake base layer and transfer into the freezer.

The only thing left is the ganachE! Simply blend all ingredients in a chopper or a blender and voila! Take out the cake, garnish it with the ganache, and bring it back in the freezer for 4 more hours and we are ready!

Raw Chocolate Cake

Ingredients:

For the base layer:
1 cup **Walnuts** (raw)
17 **Dates**
2 Tbsps. **Coconut butter** (melted)
A pinch of **Salt**

For the cream:
1 large **Avocado**
3 **Bananas**
6 Tbsps. **Cacao powder**
5 Tbsps. **Coconut butter** (melted)
5 Tbsps. **Cocoa butter** (melted)
6 **Dates**
3 Tbsps. **Maple syrup**
A pinch of **Salt**

Instructions:

First, soak the walnuts in some water for about 4 hours.

Next, strain them and wash them thoroughly.

Consecutively, dry the nuts in a dehydrator or in the oven at 50° C / 122° F.

Next, grind them finely in the kitchen chopper and leave aside 1 tablespoon for decoration.

Now, add the dates and the coconut butter and continue to blend until you have the consistency of thick dough.

Transfer the mixture into a suitable cake mold (preferably a ring) and spread it evenly to cover the whole area.

Now, we can prepare the cream, which is extremely easy.

Cut the avocado in cubes and puree it in the chopper.

Add the remaining compounds and homogenize the mixture.

Spread the cream on top of the cake and level with a spatula.

Transfer the dessert into the fridge for a few hours or overnight to harden a bit.

Finally, sprinkle with the ground walnuts and serve! Yum!

My notes:

Simple Raw Cacao Cake

Ingredients:

1 cup **Walnuts** (raw)
1 cup **Cashew** (raw)
5 Tbsps. **Cocoa butter** (melted)
5 Tbsps. **Coconut butter** (melted)
3-4 Tbsps. **Water** - optional
1/2 cup **Cacao**
2-3 Tbsps. **Maple syrup**

Instructions:

First, start by soaking the cashew in some water for at least 4 hours (or overnight).
Next, strain and wash it thoroughly.
Now, we can commence preparing the cake itself.
Grind the walnuts in a kitchen chopper or a robot.
Next, add the cocoa butter and half of the cacao.
Blend until homogeneous.
Transfer the mixture into a cake ring or a flat baking pan and spread it nicely at the bottom of the container.
Press gently to form the base layer of the cake.
Next, blend the cashew with the coconut butter and the remaining of the cacao powder.
If the consistency seems too dry, add a little bit of water to make the blending process easier.
Finally, spread the cream on top of the cake and bring the dessert in the fridge for a few hours.

Raw Fruit Cake

Ingredients:

For the base layer:
1 cup **Almonds** (raw)
1 cup **Dry cranberries**

For the cream:
1 cup **Melon**
1 cup **Coconut cream**
3-4 Tbsps. **Maple syrup** (or agave)
2 Tbsps. **Cocoa butter** (melted)

Fruits for the cream:
1 **Kiwi**
1 **Persimmon**
1 **Orange**
1/2 **Mango**
1/2 cup **Blueberries**
Several **Strawberries**

Instructions:

First, grind the almonds in a kitchen chopper.
Next, add the cranberries and homogenize the mixture.
You should have a thick and sticky mass. If not, add a little bit of water to reach that consistency.
Next, transfer the dough into a flat baking pan or a cake mold and press to form the base layer of the cake.

Melt the cocoa butter in a double boiler, if not done so already.

Now, puree the melon and blend it with the maple syrup and the coconut cream.

Add the cocoa butter and blend again.

Next, cut the fruits in medium pieces; add them to the cream, and stir.

Finally, pour the mixture in the cake mold and freeze the dessert for several hours.

Before consumption, transfer the dessert into the fridge for a little while for it to defrost, and serve!

Raw Fig Cake

Ingredients:

For the base layer:
1 cup **Walnuts** (raw)
1/2 cup **Dry figs**
2 Tbsps. **Coconut butter**
4 Tbsps. **Cacao powder**

For the cream:
1 cup **Cashew**
10 **Dates** (pitted)
1 cup **Blackberries** (fresh or frozen)
1/2 cup **Coconut butter**
1 Tbsp. **Honey** (or maple syrup for strict vegans)
Some **Desiccated coconut** – for decoration

Instructions:

First, if the blackberries are frozen, start defrosting them beforehand.

Also, soak the raw nuts and fruits separately in some clean water for several hours.

Next, strain and wash them thoroughly.

Now, we can start preparing the cake crust.

Simply blend all ingredients until homogeneous and transfer into a ring mold with approx. 8 inch diameter.

Press gently to form the base layer and transfer into the fridge to set.

Meanwhile, we can prepare the cream.

Just blend the compounds until homogeneous.

Add some water, if the consistency seems too dry and difficult to blend.

Pour the cream on top of the cake, sprinkle some coconut shreds and bring the dessert back in the fridge overnight to set.

My notes:

Raw Blueberry Chocolate Cake

Ingredients:

For the base layer:
1 cup **Walnuts** (raw)
2 Tbsps. **Maple syrup** (adjust to taste)
2 Tbsps. **Coconut butter** (melted)
3-4 Tbsps. **Cacao powder** (or carob powder)

For the chocolate cream:
3 **Bananas**
2 Tbsps. **Maple syrup**
1/4 cup **Vegan milk of choice**
6-7 Tbsps. **Cacao powder** (or carob powder)
1 Tbsp. **Sesame tahini** (or hazelnut)
3-4 Tbsps. **Coconut butter**
2 Tbsps. **Creamed coconut**

For the blueberry cream:
1 cup **Cashew** (raw)
1/2 **Lemon**
Some **Vanilla extract**
1/3 cup **Coconut butter**
Some **Maple syrup** – to taste
1 cup **Blueberries** (fresh or frozen)
A pinch of **Salt**

Instructions:

First, soak the cashew in some water overnight.

Strain the next day and wash thoroughly with clean water.

Now, we can start making the cake which is very easy and simple.

Grind the walnuts in a kitchen chopper and blend them with the remaining compounds.

Spread the mixture in a cake mold (preferably a ring mold) and press gently to form the cake crust.

Next, the second layer is the chocolate cream.

Again, simply blend all ingredients in a chopper or a kitchen robot until fully homogeneous.

Spread the cream on top of the crust and level with a spatula.

Finally – the blueberry tier.

Squeeze the juice from the lemon and blend it with the remaining ingredients.

Be careful with the berries if they are frozen – you might need to warm them slightly for the kitchen appliance to be able to puree them nicely.

Cover the cake with this purple deliciousness and put the dessert in the fridge for several hours to set.

Enjoy!

Simple Raw Blueberry Cake

Ingredients:

1 cup **Walnuts** (raw)
10 **Dates** (pitted)
2 cups **Cashew**
1 cup **Blueberries**
1 cup **Raspberries**
1/2 **Lemon**
3-4 Tbsps. **Creamed coconut**
5-6 Tbsps. **Coconut butter**
3 Tbsps. **Date molasses**

Instructions:

First, as usual, soak the cashew in some clean water for at least 2 hours.

Then, strain and wash thoroughly.

Now, we can commence making the cake!

Grind the walnuts and blend them with the dates and 3 tablespoons coconut butter.

Once you homogenize the mixture, spread it at the bottom of a cake ring.

Transfer into the fridge.

Meanwhile, we can move to the cream.

Squeeze the juice from the lemon and blend it with the remaining ingredients.

Pour the mixture on top of the cake base and bring the dessert back in the fridge for several hours to set.

Easy as that!

Raw Carrot Cake

Ingredients:

For the base layer:
4 cups **Carrot pulp**
1 1/2 cup **Dates** (pitted)
1 cup **Ground walnuts**
1 cup **Raisins**
1/2 cup **Coconut shreds**
4 Tbsps. **Coconut flour**
2 Tbsps. **Coconut butter** (soft)
Cinnamon, ginger powder, nutmeg, vanilla extract – to taste

For the cream:
1 cup **Cashew** (raw)
1/4 cup **Coconut cream**
2 Tbsps. **Maple syrup** (or agave)

Instructions:

This is a wonderful option to recycle the pulp from the delicious carrot juice!

Alternatively, you can just simply grind some carrots and the cake will become juicer.

Now, we can start with the base layer.

Place the carrot pulp in a kitchen chopper or a robot and blend it with the dates.

Next, continue adding the other compounds one by one as you stir and blend the mixture until homogeneous.

Transfer into a cake mold (preferably a cake ring) and store in the fridge for a few hours to set.

Meanwhile, we can move to the cream.

Simply blend all ingredients in a blender and we are ready to assemble the dessert!

Spread the cream on top of the cake and decorate with whatever you prefer (if you wish).

Store in the fridge for up to 3 days.

Raw Pomegranate Cake

Ingredients:

For the base layer:
1/2 cup **Raw almonds** (or almond flour)
1/2 cup **Dry cranberries**

For the cream:
1 cup **Sunflower seeds** (raw)
1 **Lemon**
3-4 Tbsps. **Maple syrup** (or agave)
1/2 cup **Dry cherries** (or blueberries)
1/2 cup **Coconut butter** (soft)
1 **Pomegranate**

For decoration:
Some **Coconut shreds**
Some **Pomegranate seeds**

Instructions:

First, soak the sunflower seeds for 2 hours.

Then, we can start preparing the cake by grinding the almonds until powdered.

Next, add the cranberries and homogenize the mixture using a chopper.

Now, take a ring mold and cover it with parchment paper.

Place the almond mixture at the bottom of the container, spread it and press to form the cake crust.

Strain the sunflower seeds and wash them thoroughly with clean water.

Transfer them into the kitchen chopper.

Next, squeeze the juice from the lemon and add it to the seeds along with the maple syrup and the dry fruits.

Blend the compounds for a few minutes until homogeneous.

Now, add the coconut butter and blend once again.

Consecutively, peel the pomegranate and remove the seeds.

Set aside some of them for the decoration, and place the rest in the mixture.

Stir with a spoon and pour the cream on top of the base layer.

Level with a spatula or a knife and place the dessert in the freezer for a couple of hours to set.

When the cake is ready, garnish with the coconut shreds and the pomegranate seeds, and serve!

Raw Coconut Cake I

Ingredients:

For the base layer:
1/2 cup **Raw almonds**
1 1/2 Tbsps. **Desiccated coconut**
2 Tbsps. **Cocoa beans**
1-2 Tbsps. **Coconut chips**
12-16 **Dates** (pitted)
2 Tbsps. **Coconut butter** (soft)
1 Tbsp. **Cocoa butter** (melted)
1 Tbsp. **Maple syrup** (or agave)
1 tsp. **Vanilla extract**

For the cream:
1 cup **Raw cashew**
1/2 cup **Desiccated coconut**
4 Tbsps. **Coconut flour**
2-3 Tbsps. **Coconut chips**
1/2 cup **Coconut cream**
6 Tbsps. **Coconut butter**
4 Tbsps. **Cocoa butter** (melted)
2-3 Tbsps. **Maple syrup** (or agave)
1 tsp. **Vanilla extract**

For decoration:
3-4 Tbsps. **Shredded cacao paste**
3-4 Tbsps. **Coconut butter**
3-4 Tbsps. **Cocoa butter** (melted)
2 Tbsps. **Maple syrup** (or agave)
1-2 Tbsps. **Coconut cream**

2 tsps. **Cacao powder**
1 tsp. **Vanilla extract**

Instructions:

Start by soaking the cashew for at least 2 hours in clean water. Continue by blending the coconut and the cocoa butters for the cake base in a double boiler.

Next, combine the almonds with the desiccated coconut, the coconut chips, and cacao beans in a kitchen chopper and grind until homogeneous.

Now, add the remaining compounds for the cake crust and homogenize the mixture. Transfer the sticky dough into a cake ring mold (with approx. 7 inch diameter) covered with parchment paper, and press to form the crust.

Now, strain the cashew and wash thoroughly. Next, grind the nuts with the coconut shreds, the coconut chips, and the coconut flour in a kitchen robot until homogeneous.

Add the remaining ingredients for the cream and blend again. Pour the sweet mass on top of the cake crust and level with a suitable utensil – a knife, a spoon, or a spatula.

Now, we can move to the chocolate topping. Melt the cocoa paste in a double boiler on low heat and blend with the two types of butter and the maple syrup.

Next, add the coconut cream, the cocoa powder, and the vanilla, and homogenize the mixture once again.

Let the chocolate cool down just a bit and pour it on top of the cake. Spread evenly and cover the dessert with kitchen foil. Transfer the cake into the fridge for at least 2 hours to set.

Release from the ring and decorate with whatever you prefer, if you wish to.

Raw Coconut Cake II (Easy Version)

Ingredients:

For the base layer:
1 1/2 cup **Coconut cream**
1/2 cup **Coconut butter**
5 Tbsps. **Maple syrup**
1/2 cup **Coconut flour**
1/2 cup **Desiccated coconut**
1-2 Tbsps. **Lemon juice**

For the chocolate icing:
2 Tbsps. **Coconut butter** (melted)
2 Tbsps. **Cacao powder**
1 Tbsp. **Maple syrup**

For decoration:
Some **Desiccated coconut**

Instructions:

This cake is extremely easy to make, but oh, so tasty!

First, simply combine all the compounds for the base layer in a kitchen chopper (or a robot) and homogenize the mixture.

Next, transfer into a cake ring (with approx. 7-8 inch diameter) and spread to cover the bottom of the container.

Sprinkle the desiccated coconut (for the decoration) on top, and place the cake in the fridge to set for a few hours.

Meanwhile, melt the coconut butter, if not done so already, and blend it with the remaining compounds for the chocolate.

Decorate the cake with the sweet brown mass and bring it back in the fridge. You can use a piping bag or a syringe to make some beautiful shapes.

Voila!

Raw Espresso Cake

Ingredients:

For the base layer:
1/2 cup **Walnuts**
3 **Dates** (pitted)
1/2 cup **Sesame flour**
2 Tbsps. **Coconut butter**
1 tsp. **Cinnamon**
A pinch of **Salt**

For the cream:
1 cup **Cashew**
1/2 cup **Vegan milk of choice**
1/2 cup **Coconut butter**
1/2 cup **Apple flour**
1 cup **Espresso**
1 **Lemon**
Some **Rum** (or rum extract)
Maple syrup – to taste

Instructions:

First, as usual, soak the cashew in some water for several hours.

Next, combine all the ingredients for the cake base in a chopper or a robot and homogenize the mixture.

Now, transfer the blend into a cake ring (with approx. 10 inch diameter) and let it chill in the fridge to set.

Meanwhile, we can continue with the cream.

Strain the cashew and wash it with clean water.

Squeeze the juice from the lemon and mix it with the nuts, the milk, some maple syrup, and the butter in a kitchen chopper.

Blend the compounds until homogeneous.

Now, divide the cream into two equal parts.

Mix one half of the mixture with some rum and pour on top of the cake base layer.

Bring the dessert in the freezer for 10 minutes.

In the meantime, mix the remaining half of the cream with the espresso and the apple flour. You may need to adjust the quantity of the flour, if the consistency becomes too liquid.

Finally, pour the dark mass on top of the cake, spread nicely with a knife (or a spatula), and bring it back in the fridge to set.

Raw Raspberry Cake

Ingredients:

For the base layer:
1 cup **Hazelnuts**
5-6 **Dates** (pitted)
A fistful of **Dry blueberries**
Some **Rum** (or water, juice) – for the blueberries
3-4 Tbsps. **Coconut butter**

For the cream:
1/2 cup **Cashew**
1 cup **Raspberries**
2-3 Tbsps. **Coconut butter**

For decoration:
3-4 Tbsps. (heaped) **Cacao powder**
3-4 Tbsps. **Coconut butter**
1/2 cup **Coconut cream**

Instructions:

We start by soaking the nuts separately (the cashew and the hazelnuts) in some water for several hours or overnight.

Also, mix the blueberries with the liquor (or juice) and let it sit for an hour or so.

Next, we can commence assembling the cake.

Strain and wash the hazelnuts and blend them with the other compounds for the cake base in a kitchen chopper or a robot.

Transfer the mixture into a cake ring (with approx. 8 inch diameter) and press to form the base layer.

Place the cake in the fridge to set.

Next, strain and wash the cashews as well and blend them with the raspberries and the butter.

Pour the cream on top of the cake and bring it back in the fridge.

Meanwhile, heat the coconut cream and the coconut butter for the icing in a double boiler.

Finally, add the cacao powder and blend until homogeneous.

Decorate the cake with the chocolate mass and let it chill for several more hours until it is completely set and firm.

My notes:

Chocolate Cake with Raspberry Delight

Ingredients:

For the base layer:
1/2 cup **Muscovado sugar**
2 Tbsps. **Hazelnut milk**
1 Tbsp. **Rum**
1/2 tsp. **Baking soda**
1 cup **Ground hazelnuts**

For the cream:
1 large **Avocado**
3 **Bananas**
1/2 cup **Agave syrup**
4 Tbsps. **Cacao powder**
1 tsp. **Maca powder**
3 Tbsps. **Coconut butter**

For the raspberry delight:
10 **Dates**
A fistful of **Raspberries**
1/2 tsp. **Pectin**

For the topping:
1/2 cup **Chocolate** (preferably sugar-free)*
3-4 Tbsps. **Vegan milk of choice**

Instructions:

Start by heating the hazelnut milk along with the rum and the brown sugar.

Stir until the sweetener fully dissolves.

Consecutively, add the baking soda and blend again.

Next, pour the mixture in a bowl with the ground hazelnuts and leave it aside to cool down.

Now, we can start making the cream.

Simply blend all ingredients until homogeneous.

Next, take a small cake ring mold and cover it with parchment paper.

Place some of the base mixture at the bottom and spread some cream on top.

Continue interchanging the layers until you are out. Remember that the cream should be at the last tier.

Bring the cake in the freezer for several hours.

Next, pit the dates and blend them with the raspberries and the pectin.

Spread the raspberry delight on top of our cake and bring it back in the freezer.

Finally, it's time for the topping.

Simply blend both ingredients in a double boiler until homogeneous.

When the cake is ready and comes out of the mold easily, garnish it with the topping and serve!

Bon appetite!

*If you do not have sugar-free chocolate at your disposal, you can always make it on your own! You can find two of my favorite healthy chocolate recipes in my FREE ebook "12 Healthy Dessert Recipes"

Mini Chocolate Fruit Cake

Ingredients:

For the base layer:
4-5 Tbsps. **Sunflower seeds**
4-5 Tbsps. **Ground walnuts**
13 **Dates** (pitted)
2-3 Tbsps. **Quinoa flakes**

For the cream:
1 cup **Cashew**
2 **Bananas**
1-2 Tbsps. **Vegan milk** (preferably vanilla flavored)
2-3 Tbsps. **Maple syrup** (or agave)
1/2 cup **Coconut butter**
1/2 cup **Strawberries**
1 Tbsp. **Bee pollen** (or desiccated coconut for strict vegans)

Instructions:

First, we need to soak the raw cashew in some water for at least 2 hours.

Now, we can commence preparing the cake.

Grind the sunflower seeds and the walnuts in a kitchen chopper.

Next, add the quinoa flakes and the dates and blend again until homogeneous.

If the fruits are too dry, you can add a little bit of water to make the blending easier.

Now, divide the mixture into two equal parts and place each one at the bottom of 2 small cake rings covered with parchment paper.

Press gently to form the cake layers and transfer them into the freezer to set.

Meanwhile, strain the cashew and wash it thoroughly with water.

Next, puree it in the kitchen chopper (or a robot) and blend it with the bananas, the maple syrup, and the vegan milk.

Now, transfer half of the cream into a cup – we will need it a bit later in the recipe.

Add half of the coconut butter in the chopper and homogenize the mixture.

Pour the cream on the first cake layer, place the second frozen tier on top of it, and bring the cake back in the freezer.

Next, blend the remaining of the cream with the strawberries and the rest of the coconut butter.

Pour the cream on top of the dessert and freeze again.

Decorate with desiccated coconut, some bee pollen or fruits before serving.

My notes:

Gluten-free Chocolate Cake with Hazelnuts

Ingredients:

For the base layer:
1 cup **Hazelnuts**
1/2 cup **Raisins**
3 Tbsps. **Coconut butter** (melted)

For the cream:
3 cups **Roasted pumpkin** (warm)
1/2 cup **Vegan milk of choice**
8 Tbsps. **Honey** (or maple syrup for strict vegans)
6 Tbsps. **Coconut butter** (melted)
6 Tbsps. **Cacao powder**
3 Tbsps. **Hazelnut tahini**
1 1/2 Tbsp. **Agar-agar**
1/2 **Vanilla pod**
A pinch of **Salt**

For decoration:
1/2 cup **Chocolate** (preferably sugar-free)*

Instructions:

First, soak the raisins in some hot water for half an hour.

Next, strain them and mix them with the hazelnuts in a kitchen chopper.

Mince and blend the ingredients well until homogeneous.

Now, transfer the dough into a cake ring and spread nicely to cover the bottom of the container.

Next, place the cake in the fridge to set.

Meanwhile, blend the pumpkin with the honey, the coconut butter, the cacao, the hazelnut tahini, and the salt in the kitchen chopper (or a robot).

At this point, you can adjust the sweetness of the mixture and add more honey or cacao powder.

Next, mix the agar with the milk and heat it in a double boiler until it melts completely.

Consecutively, add the jelly substance to the cream and homogenize the mixture once again.

Now, pour the cream on top of the cake crust and bring the dessert back in the fridge to set overnight.

Decorate with some melted chocolate before serving.

*If you do not have sugar-free chocolate at your disposal, you can always make it on your own! You can find two of my favorite healthy chocolate recipes in my FREE ebook "12 Healthy Dessert Recipes"

*Find 300+ more gluten-free recipes for the whole family and for all occasions in "The Gluten Free Cookbook Series Bundle"!

(Almost) Raw Cake for Special Occasions

Ingredients:

For the base layer:
1 cup **Raw almonds**
1/2 cup **Dry figs**
A fistful of **Pistachios** (peeled)
A fistful of **Millet popcorn**
Some **Water**

For the cream:
1 1/2 cup **Raw cashew**
1/2 cup **Blueberries**
2 **Bananas**
3-4 Tbsps. **Agave syrup**
1 **Lemon**
2 Tbsps. **Cacao powder**
1 cup **Cocoa butter** (soft)
2 tsps. **Vanilla extract**
1 cup **Vegan cookies**

For the topping:
1 cup **Coconut cream**
3 Tbsps. **Agave syrup**
2 Tbsps. **Rum**
4-5 Tbsps. **Coconut milk**

Instructions:

First, grind the almonds along with the pistachios.

Next, add the figs and a little bit of water and blend the mixture until homogeneous and sticky.

Now, add the millet popcorn and stir with a spoon.

Pour the mixture into a suitable cake mold and spread it nicely to fully cover the bottom of the container.

Next, we can continue with the cream.

Squeeze the juice from the lemon and combine it with the cashew, the agave syrup, the bananas, and the blueberries in a blender.

Blend the mixture well until homogeneous.

Next, add cacao powder, and blend again.

Add the cocoa butter as well and blend one last time.

Finally, crush the cookies, add them to the cream, and stir with a spoon.

Pour on top of the base layer and spread it evenly.

Bring the cake in the freezer to set.

Meanwhile, simply blend all the compounds for the topping and decorate the cake.

Bon appetite!

My notes:

Simple Gluten-free Cake

Ingredients:

1 cup **Rice flour**
1/2 cup **Coconut flour**
1/2 cup **Coconut sugar**
2 tsps. **Cinnamon**
1 tsp. **Baking soda**
1 tsp. **Baking powder**
1 Tbsp. **Apple cider vinegar**
1/2 tsp. **Vanilla extract**
1 **Large orange** (bio and organic)
1/3 cup **Olive oil** (or coconut butter)
Some **Nuts of choice**

Instructions:

First, squeeze the juice from the orange and grate its zest. Next, mix the dry ingredients – the 2 types of flour, the coconut sugar, cinnamon, baking powder, the orange zest, and the vanilla extract.

In another container, blend the liquids – first combine the baking soda with the apple cider vinegar, and add the orange juice, and the olive oil.

Now, combine both mixtures and homogenize the batter. Start heating the oven to 180° C/ 356° F.

Meanwhile, take a non-stick baking pan (with approx. 9 inch diameter) and pour the batter in.

Arrange the nuts on top and bake the dessert until fully cooked (when the toothpick comes out clean).

Apple Chocolate Cake

Ingredients:

2 **Bananas** (fully ripe)
1/2 cup **Vegan chocolate***
1 1/4 cup **All-purpose wholegrain flour**
1/2 cup **Coconut sugar**
1/4 cup **Muscovado sugar**
1/4 cup **Cacao powder**
1/2 cup **Apple puree**
1 tsp. **Baking soda**
1/4 tsp. **Salt**
1/3 cup **Water**
1 tsp. **White vinegar** (or apple cider vinegar)

Instructions:

First, mash the bananas in a bowl.

Next, add the two types of sugar, the apple puree, the water, and the vinegar.

Blend the compounds until fully homogeneous.

Now, combine the dry ingredients in another container – the flour, baking soda, the cacao, and the salt.

If you are using store-bought chocolate bar, chop it in chunks and add half of it to the dry ingredients mix.

Next, slowly transfer the mixture into the bowl with the liquids as you stir and homogenize the batter.

At this point, you can start heating the oven to 180° C/ 356° F.

Now, pour the batter in a non-stick baking mold (with about 8 inch diameter) and sprinkle the remaining of the chocolate at the top.

If you do not have a non-stick pan, you can just grease a regular pan and cover it with flour before pouring the batter.

Place the cake at the oven floor and bake until fully cooked and the toothpick comes out clean.

Wait for the dessert to cool down completely before cutting and serving.

*If you do not have sugar-free chocolate at your disposal, you can always make it on your own! You can find two of my favorite healthy chocolate recipes in my FREE ebook "12 Healthy Dessert Recipes"

My notes:

No-bake Apple Cake

Ingredients:

For the chocolate layer:
1/2 cup **Vegan chocolate*** (preferably sugar-free)
3-4 Tbsps. **Vegan milk of choice**
5 Tbsps. **Ground hazelnuts**

For the apple layer:
1 average **Apple**
1/2 cup **Fine oatmeal**
1/2 cup **Desiccated coconut**
1/2 cup **Banana chips**
2 Tbsps. **Almond flour**
2 Tbsps. **Coconut sugar**
1 Tbsp. **Coconut butter**
1/2 cup **Raisins**

Instructions:

We can start by heating the milk in a double boiler on low temperature.

Next, add the chocolate and stir until it melts and blends with the milk.

Now, add the hazelnuts, blend again, and take the mixture off the heat.

Take a ring mold and cover it with parchment paper.
Pour the mixture in to form the base layer of the cake.
Transfer into the fridge for a few hours to set.
Meanwhile, we can continue with the fruit layer.

Remove the seeds from the apple and mince the fruit in a kitchen chopper or a blender.

Next, add the oatmeal, the desiccated coconut, the banana chips, and the almond flour.

Blend until homogeneous.

Consecutively, add the butter and homogenize the mixture once again.

Finally, add the raisins and stir the cream with a spoon.

Now, pour the apple layer on top of the chocolate one and bring the dessert back in the fridge to set.

*If you do not have sugar-free chocolate at your disposal, you can always make it on your own! You can find two of my favorite healthy chocolate recipes in my FREE ebook "12 Healthy Dessert Recipes"

My notes:

No-bake Almond Cake with Pumpkin Cream

Ingredients:

For the base layer:
1/4 cup **Almonds**
1/4 cup **Dry cranberries** (or blueberries)
1 Tbsp. **Chia**
3-4 **Dates** (pitted)
1 tsp. **Vanilla extract**

For the pumpkin cream:
2 cups **Pumpkin** (steamed, roasted, boiled)
2-3 Tbsps. **Cacao powder**
1 tsp. **Vanilla extract**

Instructions:

First, grind the almonds and the cranberries in a kitchen chopper.

Next, blend them with the remaining compounds for the base layer.

Transfer the mixture into a cake ring or a casserole covered with parchment paper.

Press to form the cake crust.

Now, blend the pumpkin with the cacao and the vanilla extract.

If you prefer the cream to be sweeter, you can add some dates or maple syrup and blend again until homogeneous.

Pour the mixture on top of the cake and place the dessert in the fridge for a few hours to set.

Carrot Cake

Ingredients:

For the base layer:
2-3 **Carrots**
1/2 cup **Walnuts**
1/2 cup **Ground flax seeds**
1 Tbsp. **Cinnamon**
1 tsp. **Baking powder**
3 Tbsps. **Cocoa butter** (melted)
10 **Dates** (pitted)

For the cream:
1 cup **Cashew**
1 tsp. **Vanilla extract**
2 Tbsps. **Maple syrup**
Some **Vegan milk of choice** (or water)

Instructions:

First, soak the cashew in some water for at least 2 hours.

Next, strain and wash thoroughly.

Now, we can commence preparing the cake itself.

Grate the carrots or mince them in a kitchen chopper until pureed.

Next, grind the walnuts and blend them with the flax seeds, the cinnamon, and the baking powder.

Transfer the mixture into a large bowl.

Now, blend the dates with the melted butter in the chopper.

Combine all ingredients for the cake base in the bowl – the grated carrots, the date puree, and the walnuts.

Transfer the batter into a baking pan covered with parchment paper.

Heat the oven to 180° C/ 356° F and bake for about 40 minutes.

Meanwhile, we can prepare the cream.

Puree the soaked cashew and blend it with the vanilla and the maple syrup.

Next, add some milk or water and continue to homogenize the cream.

Add as much liquid as to reach the desired thick consistency.

When the cake crust is ready and cooled down, cover it with the cashew cream and serve!

My notes:

Raw Cheesecake

Ingredients:

For the base layer:
1 **Banana**
10 **Dates**
1 cup **Raw almonds**

For the cream:
2 cups **Cashew**
1 tsp. **Vanilla**
1/2 **Lemon**
1/2 cup **Water**
3 Tbsps. **Honey** (maple syrup for a strictly vegan recipe)

Instructions:

Start by pitting the dates and blending them with the banana and the almonds. Use a kitchen chopper or a robot to reach a homogeneous consistency.

Next, transfer the mixture into a ring mold and press gently to form the base layer. Place it in the freezer for about 15 minutes to harden a bit and maintain its shape.

Next, repeat the same with the cream – squeeze the juice from the lemon and blend it with the remaining compounds in a kitchen chopper until you are happy with the consistency.

Pour the mixture on top of the cheesecake crust and bring it back in the freezer for 60 more minutes.

Finally, decorate with whatever you prefer and serve!

Raw Strawberry Cheesecake

Ingredients:

For the base layer:
1/2 cup **Almonds**
1/4 cup **Brazil nuts**
2 Tbsps. **Ground black cumin seeds**
1/2 tsp. **Salt**
1 tsp. **Grated lemon zest** (organic, bio)
10 **Dates** (pitted)

For the cream:
1 cup **Cashew**
1 cup **Strawberries**
3 Tbsps. **Lemon juice**
4 Tbsps. **Maple syrup**
1/2 tsp. **Salt**
1 tsp. **Vanilla extract**
4 Tbsps. **Coconut butter** (soft)

For decoration:
3-4 Tbsps. **Coconut butter**
3-4 Tbsps. **Water**
4 Tbsps. **Cacao powder**
3 Tbsps. **Maple syrup**
1/2 tsp. **Salt**

Instructions:

First, we need to prepare some of the ingredients for this recipe. Soak the cashew in some water for at least 2 hours.

Also, soak the dates in water, fresh juice or some amaretto (or nocino) for at least 30 minutes, especially if the fruits are not juicy enough.

Next, grind the almonds in a kitchen chopper along with the brazil nuts, the salt, and the black cumin.

Now, add the soaked dates and homogenize the mixture once again. Add the liquid in which the fruits have been soaking, if you wish to make the cheesecake crust juicier.

Transfer the mixture into a cake ring mold and press to form the base layer. Place the cake in the fridge to set while we continue with the cream.

Now, strain the cashew and wash it thoroughly with water.

Next, grind it in the chopper and blend with the other ingredients (except the coconut butter).

Once the mixture is fully homogenous, add the butter and blend again. Pour the cream on top of the crust and spread evenly with a spatula.

Bring the dessert back in the fridge for 6 hours to set completely.

Finally, when the cake is ready, blend all the compounds for the decoration with a hand blender until homogeneous.

Garnish the cheesecake with the chocolate and when it hardens (due to the low temperature of the cake), cut the dessert and serve!

Marzipan Mini Cakes

Ingredients:

For the marzipan:
1 cup **Creamed coconut**
1 cup **Almond milk**
3-4 Tbsps. **Agave syrup**
3-4 Tbsps. **Cocoa butter** (melted)
4 Tbsps. **Ground almonds**
1 cup **Almond flour**
4 Tbsps. **Amaretto** (or Nocino)

For the chocolate base:
1/2 cup **Vegan chocolate** (preferably sugar-free)*

For the topping:
1/2 cup **Vegan chocolate** (preferably sugar-free)*
2 Tbsps. **Almond milk**

Instructions:

First, we start with the marzipan!

Place the creamed coconut, the almond milk, and the agave syrup in a blender and homogenize the mixture.

Next, add the cocoa butter and the ground almonds. Stir with a spoon and transfer the mixture into a cake mold covered with parchment paper.

Place the dessert in the fridge until it sets.

Now, take it out, remove the paper, and chop it in small pieces.

Blend with the almond flour and the amaretto liquor until homogeneous.

Next, take your favorite mini cake molds (or muffin molds) and divide the marzipan into each container.

Press to form the base layer of the desserts.

Bring them back in the fridge to maintain the forms.

Meanwhile, we can start making the chocolate and the topping.

Simply melt the chocolate (1/2 cup) in a double boiler, spread it on one side of the cakes, and let it harden.

Next, melt the other half of the chocolate and mix it with the almond milk.

Flip the desserts, so that the chocolate layer remains at the bottom and decorate with the topping.

That's it!

*If you do not have sugar-free chocolate at your disposal, you can always make it on your own! You can find two of my favorite healthy chocolate recipes in my FREE ebook "12 Healthy Dessert Recipes"

My notes:

No-bake Chestnut Mini Cake

Ingredients:

3-4 Tbsps. **Pumpkin seed protein**
1 cup **Chestnut spread*** (sugar-free)
1 **Avocado**
3-4 Tbsps. **Vegan chocolate**** (melted)
1/2 cup **Walnuts** (or pecans)

Instructions:

Take a small cake mold and cover it with parchment paper. Sprinkle half of the pumpkin protein at the bottom of the pan. Melt the chocolate in a double boiler, if not done so already.

Meanwhile, mash the avocado and blend it with the chestnut cream.

Next, grind the walnuts and add them to the chestnut mixture. Stir and homogenize the cream, and pour it in the cake mold. Finally, sprinkle the rest of the pumpkin seed protein on top and freeze the cake for several hours.

*If you do not have sugar-free chestnut spread, you can substitute with homemade hazelnut cream – find the recipe in the Pudding and Cream Recipes section below.

**If you do not have sugar-free chocolate at your disposal, you can always make it on your own! You can find two of my favorite healthy chocolate recipes in my FREE ebook "12 Healthy Dessert Recipes"

Orange Tart

Ingredients:

For the tart:
1 cup **Oatmeal**
5-6 Tbsps. **Coconut flour**
2 Tbsps. **Sesame tahini**
5-6 Tbsps. **Water**
1 tsp. **Baking soda**
Coconut sugar – to taste

For the orange cream:
2 cups **Fresh orange juice**
4 tsps. **Corn starch**
2 tsps. **Agar-agar powder**
Coconut sugar – to taste
Some **Water**

Instructions:

First, grind the oatmeal finely.

Next, blend it with the remaining ingredients to reach homogeneous non-sticky dough.

Adjust the quantities of the oatmeal and the water to reach the desired consistency, if needed.

Now, take a medium-sized tart pan or several smaller ones and spread the dough at the bottom and the walls of the mold.

Poke a few holes at the bottom of the tart and heat the oven to 180° C/ 356° F.

Bake the base for our dessert for about 15 minutes.

Meanwhile, we can continue with the cream.

Heat the orange juice in a metal pot.

In the meantime, blend the starch, the coconut sugar, and the agar with some water and stir until you have a nice homogeneous mass.

When the juice starts simmering, add the starch mixture and stir until the cream thickens.

Leave it aside as you wait for the baked tart to cool down completely.

Next, pour the cream at the center of the pastry and transfer the dessert into the freezer for about 30 minutes (until the cream gelatinizes).

That's it!

My notes:

Flour-less Fruit Tarts

Ingredients:

For the base:
4 Tbsps. **Desiccated coconut**
4 Tbsps. **Almond flour**
1 Tbsp. **Cacao powder**
1 Tbsp. **Maple syrup**
1 Tbsp. **Cocoa butter** (melted)

For the cream:
1/2 cup **Creamed coconut**
1/2 cup **Almond cream**
2 Tbsps. **Maple syrup**
1 Tbsp. **Rum**
1 Tbsp. **Ground flax seeds**
A pinch of **Salt**

Fruits of choice

Instructions:

First, blend the products for the tart bases in a kitchen chopper or a robot.

Next, divide it into several tart molds and press gently to form the crust. Now, arrange some cut fruits of your choice in each cup – peaches, pineapple, blueberries, etc.

Finally, blend the compounds for the cream and pour it on top of the fruits.

Bring the desserts in the freezer until they set and remove from the molds.

MUFFINS AND BROWNIES

Chocolate Muffins with Sweet Potato

Ingredients:

1 **Sweet potato** (large)
1/2 cup **Maple syrup**
5 Tbsps. **Coconut butter** (melted)
1 1/2 tsp. **Vanilla extract**
1/2 cup **Rice milk**
1 cup **Chickpea flour**
1 cup **Coconut flour**
1/4 tsp. **Salt**
4 tsps. **Baking powder**
3-4 Tbsps. **Cocoa powder**
1/2 cup **Dark chocolate** (sugar-free)*

Instructions:

First, peel the sweet potato, cut it in small pieces and boil it until it softens.

Next, strain it and mash it nicely with a fork.

Add the maple syrup, the coconut butter, vanilla extract, and the rice milk. Blend everything well.

In another container, mix the dry ingredients – chickpea flour, coconut flour, salt, baking powder, and the cocoa powder. Stir well to blend them as well.

Next, combine both mixtures and use a hand mixer to homogenize the batter completely until it forms thick dough.

Melt the chocolate in a double boiler and prepare the muffin molds (about 12 pieces).

Place a paper cupcake cup in each muffin mold and one tablespoon of the dough.

Next, pour one tablespoon of the melted chocolate in each cup, and divide the remaining dough in each muffin cup.

Now, it is time to heat the oven at 200° C/ 392° F and bake the desserts for 8 minutes. Finally, lower the temperature to 180° C/ 356° F and continue cooking the muffins for 10-15 more minutes.

*If you do not have sugar-free chocolate at your disposal, you can always make it on your own! You can find two of my favorite healthy chocolate recipes in my FREE ebook "12 Healthy Dessert Recipes"

"

No-bake Cocoa Oatmeal Muffins

Ingredients:

1 cup **Oatmeal**
2 Tbsps. **Cocoa powder**
1 cup **Coconut butter**
1 cup **Ground walnuts**
1/2 cup **Molasses**
1 tsp. **Vanilla extract**

Instructions:

First, melt the butter and mix it with the molasses. Blend well.

Next, in another bowl, mix the oatmeal with the cocoa powder.

Transfer the oatmeal mixture to the butter and molasses, and blend them as well.

Finally, add the walnuts and the vanilla extract, and stir one more time.

Place some of the mixture in muffin molds and put them in the fridge. The butter will stiffen and keep the form of the muffins.

Note: if you wish to improve the taste of the oatmeal and the walnuts, you can roast them in a non-stick pan for several minutes before preparing the desserts.

My notes:

No-bake Fig Muffins

Ingredients:

1 cup **Raw almonds**
1 1/2 cup **Dry figs**
1 **Lemon** (organic, bio)
Some **Fruit jam of choice** – blueberry, rosehip, strawberry, etc. (preferably homemade and sugar-free)
1 tsp. **Vanilla extract**

Instructions:

First, grate the lemon zest.
Next, grind the almonds in a kitchen chopper.
Add the figs and blend until fully homogeneous.
Then, add the lemon zest and the vanilla extract and stir one last time.
Divide the mixture into muffin cups and make a hole at the center of each dessert.
Fill the crater with 1-2 tablespoons of jam and refrigerate for a few hours.
Easy as that!

My notes:

Egg-less Muffins

Ingredients:

1 cup **Almond tahini**
6 Tbsps. **Carob powder**
1/2 cup **Almond flour**
1 cup **Vegan milk** (almond, coconut, etc.)
3-4 Tbsps. **Maple syrup** (adjust to taste)

Instructions:

This is a very fast and easy recipe, so you can start by heating the oven to 180° C/ 356° F.

Next, simply blend all ingredients until fully homogeneous.

You can add more milk, if the batter seems too thick.

Pour into a muffin tin (with 12 cups) and bake until fully cooked!

Voila!

My notes:

Gluten-free Muffins

Ingredients:

1 cup **Orange juice**
1 cup **Chickpea flour**
3-4 Tbsps. **Desiccated coconut**
3-4 Tbsps. **Corn flour** (non-GMO)
3 Tbsps. **Coconut butter**
1 cup **Dates** (pitted)
1/2 tsp. **Baking soda**
Cinnamon – to taste

Instructions:

Start heating the oven to 180° C/ 356° F.

Meanwhile, grind and blend all ingredients in a kitchen chopper or a robot until fully homogeneous.

You can add more water or flour to reach the desired consistency of cake batter.

Pour into muffin molds and bake until fully cooked! Voila!

*Find 300+ more gluten-free recipes for the whole family and for all occasions in "The Gluten Free Cookbook Series Bundle"!

Raw Muffins I

Ingredients:

1 cup **Coconut butter** (soft)
2 1/2 Tbsps. **Cacao powder**
3 Tbsps. **Honey** (or maple syrup for strict vegans)
3 Tbsps. **Desiccated coconut**
3 Tbsps. **Goji berries**
20 **Dates** (pitted)
1/3 cup **Almonds**
2 Tbsps. **Coconut sugar**

Instructions:

First, we need to soak the dates in some warm water, or fresh fruit juice, or maybe some rum, if you are feeling naughty.

In about half an hour we can proceed with the muffins and the technology is plain and simple.

Combine all compounds in a kitchen chopper, a robot, or a blender.

Mince and homogenize the mixture completely.

Pour the batter into muffin molds and transfer into the fridge for a few hours to set.

Enjoy!

Raw Muffins II

Ingredients:

1/2 cup **Tahini** (sesame, hazelnut, walnut, etc.)
2 Tbsps. **Maple syrup**
2 Tbsps. **Coconut butter**
3 Tbsps. **Desiccated coconut**
2 Tbsps. **Cacao powder**
2 fistfuls of **Raw sunflower seeds** (peeled)
1 **Banana** (fully ripe)

Instructions:

This is another unbelievably easy but tasty recipe!

All you need to do is blend all the compounds in a kitchen chopper until fully homogeneous.

Next, pour the mixture into muffin molds and freeze for a few hours.

Release from the molds and serve right before consumption.

This is an excellent sugar-free summer treat!

My notes:

Apple Brownie

Ingredients:

For the base:
2/3 cup **Buckwheat flakes**
1 cup **Ground almonds** (raw or blanched)
4 Tbsps. **Apple flour**
2 **Large apples**
2 Tbsps. **Coconut butter** (soft)
1 tsp. **Almond extract**
Some **Date molasses** – to taste
Some **Water** (for the apples)

For the icing:
2 Tbsps. **Hazelnut tahini**
2 Tbsps. **Sesame tahini**
2 Tbsps. **Honey** (maple syrup for strict vegans) – adjust to taste
1 Tbsp. **Cocoa powder** (or carob powder)
3 1/2 – 4 Tbsps. **Coconut butter**
1/2 cup **Coconut cream**

Instructions:

First, cut the apples in quarters and boil them in some water until they soften.

Next, when the fruits cool down, remove the seeds and cut the apples in small pieces.

Important: do not throw away the apple broth – we will need it later in the recipe!

Consecutively, mix all ingredients for the base of the brownie in a kitchen robot, a chopper or a blender.

Blend them well and add some of the apple water to reach the desired consistency – a thick mass.

Start heating the oven to the usual 180° C/ 356° F.

Next, pour the cake batter in a baking pan (approx. 11" x 7") covered with parchment paper.

Cook for about 40-45 minutes until fully baked.

In the meantime, we can make the topping.

Place all the components for the cream in a double boiler and blend them on low heat.

Remember to keep the temperature below 98.6°F (37°C) to preserve the beneficial nutrients in the honey.

Otherwise, you can use maple syrup, or wait for the cream to cool down a bit before adding the bee product!

When the brownie is ready and nicely chilled, remove it from the baking pan and cover with the tahini topping!

My notes:

Flour-less Brownies

Ingredients:

4 **Bananas**
1/2 cup **Hazelnut tahini** (or sesame)
2-3 Tbsps. **Cacao powder**
1 tsp. **Baking powder**
A pinch of **Salt**
1 tsp. **Vanilla extract**
Some **Vegan chocolate*** – to taste

Instructions:

This recipe is very simple!

Mash the bananas and blend them with the remaining ingredients.

Remember to leave some of the chocolate for decoration.

Pour the mixture into a baking pan and sprinkle the chocolate bits on top.

Next, heat the oven to 180° C/ 356° F and bake for about 20 minutes until fully cooked.

Finally, wait for the dessert to cool down completely and cut it in pieces.

Store in the fridge.

*If you do not have sugar-free chocolate at your disposal, you can always make it on your own! You can find two of my favorite healthy chocolate recipes in my FREE ebook "12 Healthy Dessert Recipes"

Flour-less Coffee Brownies (Energy Bars)

Ingredients:

1 cup **Nuts of choice** (almonds, walnuts, hazelnuts, etc.)
1/2 cup **Dates** (pitted)
2 Tbsps. **Cacao powder**
1 Tbsp. **Instant coffee** (or instant chicory coffee substitute)
1 Tbsp. **Coconut butter** (or melted cocoa butter)
A pinch of **Salt**

Instructions:

Grind the nuts in a kitchen chopper.

Next, add the remaining compounds and blend the mixture until fully homogeneous.

Now, transfer the sweet mass into a flat pan covered with parchment paper and spread it evenly.

Press to form a tight layer and refrigerate for several hours until it sets.

Finally, cut in the desired shapes and enjoy!

My notes:

Batata Brownies I

Ingredients:

2 **Batatas** (sweet potatoes)
1/2 cup **Walnuts**
3 Tbsps. **Coconut butter** (soft)
2 Tbsps. **Carob powder**
1 tsp. **Cinnamon**
Some **Vegan chocolate*** – for decoration

Instructions:

First, heat the oven to 180° C/ 356° F. Poke several holes in the potatoes and roast them for about 40 minutes until fully cooked.

Next, leave them aside to cool down, peel them, and mash them with a potato masher or a fork.

Now, grind the walnuts in a kitchen chopper and mix them with the potato puree. Add the remaining compounds and blend until homogeneous. Transfer the mixture into a flat baking pan and cook for about 20 minutes (you can switch on the fan, if you have it).

Meanwhile, grate the chocolate. When the dessert is ready, garnish with the chocolate shreds while still hot to let it melt a bit. Cut in the desired shapes and sizes, and enjoy!

*If you do not have sugar-free chocolate at your disposal, you can always make it on your own! You can find two of my favorite healthy chocolate recipes in my FREE ebook "12 Healthy Dessert Recipes"

Batata Brownies II

Ingredients:

1 1/2 cup **Roasted batatas** (sweet potatoes)
1 1/2 cup **Buckwheat flakes**
1 1/2 cup **Ground almonds**
16 **Dates** (pitted)
3 Tbsps. **Beet syrup**
1/4 cup **Cacao powder**
1/4 cup **Carob powder**
3-4 Tbsps. **Coconut butter**
2/3 of 13.5 oz. can **Coconut cream**
Some **Hot water** - optional
Some **Vegan chocolate*** – for decoration

Instructions:

You can start by heating the oven to 180° C/ 356° F.

Next, puree the batatas in a kitchen chopper or a robot.

Then, start adding the compounds one by one as you continue to blend the mixture.

If the batter seems too dry, add some hot water to reach a creamy consistency.

Next, pour in a baking mold covered with parchment paper and bake for about 40-45 minutes until fully cooked.

When the dessert is ready and cooled down, melt the chocolate and spread it on top of the cake.

Transfer into the fridge for a few hours to set and cut in the desired shapes and sizes.

Enjoy!

COOKIES AND BISCUITS

Simple Biscuits

Ingredients:

2 cups **Fine oatmeal**
1 tsp. **Cinnamon**
1/4 tsp. **Vanilla powder**
1 **Apple**
A fistful of **Raisins**

Instructions:

Peel the apple, remove its seeds and grind the fruit in a kitchen chopper.

Next, simply combine all ingredients and blend them with a spoon.

Leave the mixture to rest for about 30 minutes.

Next, take a baking tray and cover it with parchment paper.

Form the biscuits with the spoon and bake at 180° C/ 356° F for about 20 minutes.

Voila!

My notes:

Gluten-free Cinnamon Cookies

Ingredients:

1 cup **Buckwheat flour**
1/2 cup **Coconut butter** (melted)
5 Tbsps. **Vegan milk**
5 Tbsps. **Maple syrup** (or agave)
1 tsp. **Baking powder**
1/2 tsp. **Baking soda**
1 tsp. **Ginger powder**
1 tsp. **Cinnamon**
1/4 tsp. **Nutmeg**

Instructions:

First, melt the coconut butter in a double boiler, if not done so already.

Next, mix the dry ingredients in a bowl – the flour, baking powder, baking soda, and the spices.

In another container, blend the liquids – the butter, the sweetener, and the nut milk.

Next, start slowly and carefully combining both mixtures as you stir with a hand mixer (or a blender).

The goal is to reach non-sticky dough. If needed, add more flour to reach that consistency.

Place the mixture in the fridge for about 10 minutes to rest.

Now, take some parchment paper and roll out the dough in a thin layer on top of it.

Cut the cookies in the desired shapes and sizes.

At this point, you can start heating the oven to 180° C/ 356° F.

Next, take a baking pan, cover it with the parchment paper, and arrange the biscuits in it.

Bake for about 10 minutes until golden.

Finally, leave the desserts to cool down for several hours before consuming!

Bon appetite!

Find 300+ more gluten-free recipes for the whole family and for all occasions in "The Gluten Free Cookbook Series Bundle"!

Blueberry Cookies

Ingredients:

2 **Bananas**
10 **Dates** (pitted)
2-3 Tbsps. **Blueberry jam** (preferably homemade and sugar-free)
1 cup **Coconut milk**
1 cup **Apple flour**
1/2 cup **Rice flour**
1/2 tsp. **Baking powder**
1 Tbsp. **Chia**
2-3 Tbsps. **Coconut butter** (melted)
4 1/2 Tbsps. **Ground hazelnuts**
1-2 tsps. **Vanilla extract**
2-3 fistfuls of **Fresh blueberries**

Instructions:

Start heating the oven to 180° C/ 356° F.

In the meantime, we will prepare the cookie dough since the procedure is very easy and quick.

Cut the bananas in medium pieces and place them in a kitchen robot or a blender.

Add the remaining ingredients (except the whole blueberries) and blend well until they fully homogenize.

Add the fresh berries and gently stir with a spoon or a spatula to distribute them evenly.

Take a baking tray and cover it with parchment paper.

Form the cookies as usual – shape them as small spheres and press gently to flatten the biscuits.

Bake for about 20-30 minutes until they are fully cooked and ready!

Enjoy!

My notes:

Pumpkin Cookies Variation I (Gluten-free)

Ingredients:

1 cup **Roasted pumpkin puree**
3-4 Tbsps. **Coconut butter** (melted)
1 **Orange** (organic, bio)
2 Tbsps. **Coconut sugar**
1/2 cup **Gluten-free flour of choice**
1 tsp. **Baking soda**
1 tsp. **Cinnamon**
1/4 tsp. **Salt**

Instructions:

Start heating the oven to 190° C/ 374° F. In the meantime, squeeze the juice from the citrus fruit and grate the zest.

Next, combine the pumpkin puree with the coconut butter, 1 tablespoon of the juice, the orange zest, and the coconut sugar. Stir and blend the ingredients well.

Consecutively, add the remaining compounds one by one as you continue to homogenize the mixture.

Now, take a baking pan and cover it with parchment paper. Scoop from the cookie dough, form the desserts, and arrange them in the container. Bake for about 10-15 minutes until golden.

*Find 300+ more gluten-free recipes for the whole family and for all occasions in "The Gluten Free Cookbook Series Bundle"!

Pumpkin Cookies Variation II (Flourless)

Ingredients:

1 cup **Roasted pumpkin puree**
3-4 Tbsps. **Cashew puree**
1 **Orange** (organic, bio)
2 Tbsps. **Coconut sugar**
1/2 cup **Desiccated coconut**
1 tsp. **Baking soda**
1 tsp. **Cinnamon**
1/4 tsp. **Salt**

Instructions:

Note: prepare the cashew puree by soaking raw cashew nuts for several hours and then, grinding them in a kitchen chopper.

The technology for preparing these delicious cookies is the same as the previous variation.

Simply combine the pumpkin puree with the cashews, the orange juice, the zest, and the coconut sugar.

Blend this mixture with the remaining ingredients and homogenize again.

Form the cookies and place them in a baking tray covered with parchment paper.

Bake for 10-15 minutes in a hot oven at 190° C/ 374° F.

Let the desserts cool down on a grid and store them in a tightly-sealed jar for up to 3-4 days.

Avocado Cookies

Ingredients:

1/2 cup **Avocado** (ripe)
1/2 cup **Coconut sugar**
1/2 tsp. **Vanilla extract**
1 tsp. **Apple cider vinegar**
1/2 tsp. **Baking powder**
2 Tbsps. **Cocoa powder**
1 tsp. **Cinnamon**
3/4 cup **Wholegrain flour of choice** (or gluten-free)
1/2 cup **Dark chocolate chips** (preferably sugar-free)

Instructions:

Begin by heating the oven to 180° C/ 356° F.

Next, mash the avocado and blend it with the sugar.

Consecutively, add the vanilla extract, the cinnamon, the apple cider vinegar, the cocoa powder, the baking powder, and stir again nicely.

Finally, add the flour and blend completely until the mixture becomes fully homogenous.

Add the chocolate chips and stir again with a spoon.

Shape the cookies as usual – scoop some of the dough, place the balls on the baking tray (covered with parchment paper), and press them.

Bake the desserts for 15-20 minutes until they are fully cooked.

Leave them to cool down completely before sealing them in your favorite cookie jar!

Apricot Cookies

Ingredients:

1/2 cup **Dry apricots**
1/2 cup **Sunflower seeds**
2 Tbsps. **Sesame seeds**
2 Tbsps. **Golden linseed**
2 Tbsps. **Desiccated coconut**
1/3 tsp. **Nutmeg**
1/2 **Orange** (organic, bio)
1 Tbsp. **Cocoa butter** (melted)
Some **Coconut cream** – for decoration

Instructions:

First, squeeze the juice from the orange and grate the zest.

Next, mix the citrus juice with the apricots in a chopper and homogenize the mixture.

Then, add the zest, the sunflower seeds, the sesame seeds, flax seeds, the coconut shreds, and the nutmeg.

Stir the batter until fully homogeneous.

Now, add the cocoa butter and blend one last time.

Finally, form the cookies and arrange them in a tray.

Decorate with some coconut cream and refrigerate for a few hours to set.

No-bake Maple Syrup Cookies

Ingredients:

For the cookies:
1/2 cup **Maple syrup**
1 cup **Coconut sugar**
2 Tbsps. **Water**
1/2 tsp. **Baking soda**
1 cup **Almond flour**
1 tsp. **Cinnamon**
1/2 tsp. **Ground clove buds**

For the topping:
1/2 cup **Vegan chocolate***
10-15 **Raw nuts of choice** (walnuts, almonds, hazelnuts, etc.)

Instructions:

First, mix the maple syrup, the coconut sugar and the water in a metal pot and heat them on low temperature.

Next, add the baking soda and continue stirring the mixture.

Be careful not to let it burn!

When the mixture starts bulging up, add the almond flour and the spices.

You will have nice soft sweet dough – the base for our cookies.

Start forming small balls and press them gently to make the desserts flatter.

Transfer them in the fridge for about half an hour to cool down.

Meanwhile, melt the chocolate in a double boiler.

Finally, spread some of the dark brown mass on top of the cookies and place a nut on each biscuit.

Voila!

*If you do not have sugar-free chocolate at your disposal, you can always make it on your own! You can find two of my favorite healthy chocolate recipes in my FREE ebook "12 Healthy Dessert Recipes"

Banana Cookies

Ingredients:

1/2 cup **Coconut butter** (soft)
2 **Bananas** (ripe)
1/2 cup **Dates** (pitted)
1/2 cup **Chickpea flour**
1 cup **Rice flour**
1 Tbsp. **Cinnamon**
1 tsp. **Baking powder**
3 Tbsps. **Ground flax seeds**
2-3 Tbsps. **Dark chocolate chips** (preferably sugar-free)

Instructions:

Simply blend all ingredients completely in a kitchen robot (a blender, or a chopper).

The final result should be nice non-sticky cookie dough.

If not, add some more rice flour and blend again.

Next, you can start heating the oven to 170° C/338° F.

After that, take a baking tray and cover it with parchment paper.

Form the biscuits as usual – shape them as small balls and press to make them flatter.

Bake the desserts for about 12-15 minutes. If you like them crunchier, leave them to get a nice golden crust at the top.

Voila!

My notes:

Apple Cookies

Ingredients:

1 cup **Apple flour**
1/2 cup **Rice flour**
1 Tbsp. **Chia seeds**
1 cup **Vegan milk of choice** (coconut, rice, hemp, etc.)
2 **Bananas** (fully ripe)
1/2 tsp. **Baking powder**
10 **Dates** (pitted)
Cinnamon – to taste
5 Tbsps. **Ground walnuts**
2 Tbsps. **Maple syrup** - optional

Instructions:

These tasty cookies are very easy to make but extremely delicious.

They do not contain any additional fat, but you can prepare them with some coconut butter, if you desire.

First, mix the two types of flour with the baking powder and blend nicely.

Next, add the chia seeds and the milk, and stir again.

Consecutively, mash the bananas and mince the dates in small pieces.

Now, add the fruits to the main mixture along with the cinnamon and the ground nuts.

If you prefer the cookies to be sweeter, add some maple syrup.

Homogenize the batter and leave it aside to rest for about 10 minutes for the chia seeds to absorb some of the liquid.

Meanwhile, start heating the oven to 180° C/ 356° F with a fan.

Finally, form the cookies, arrange them on a baking pan covered with parchment paper, and bake for about 15 minutes until fully cooked.

Pear Cookies

Ingredients:

1 cup **Pears** (fully ripe and sweet)
1/2 cup **Coconut butter** (soft)
1/2 cup **Maple syrup** (or molasses)
1/2 cup **Chickpea flour**
1 cup **Corn flour** (non-GMO)
3-4 Tbsps. **Ground walnuts**
3-4 Tbsps. **Oat bran**
1 tsp. **Baking powder**
A pinch of **Salt**
1 tsp. **Ginger powder**
1 tsp. **Cinnamon**
1/2 cup **Vegan chocolate*** (preferably sugar-free)

Instructions:

First, remove the seeds from the pears and puree the fruits.

Next, place the coconut butter in a kitchen chopper or a robot and blend it with the salt, the ginger powder, and the cinnamon.

Add the maple syrup and the pear puree and blend again until homogeneous.

Transfer the mixture into a bowl and combine with the chickpea flour, the corn meal, and the oat bran.

Next, add the chocolate (if you are using a store-bought chocolate bar, chop it into pieces) to the cookie dough along with the walnuts.

Start heating the oven to 180° C/ 356° F.

Take a baking tray and cover it with parchment paper.

Form the cookies with the desired shapes and sizes and bake for about 15 minutes until golden.

*If you do not have sugar-free chocolate at your disposal, you can always make it on your own! You can find two of my favorite healthy chocolate recipes in my FREE ebook "12 Healthy Dessert Recipes"

My notes:

Festive Ginger Cookies

Ingredients:

3 1/2 cups **Wholegrain flour**
1/2 tsp. **Baking powder**
1 tsp. **Cinnamon**
1/2 tsp. **Nutmeg**
1/2 cup **Coconut butter** (soft)
1/2 **Banana**
2 1/2 tsps. **Grated ginger root**
1/2 cup **Maple syrup** (or molasses, agave, stevia, etc.)
15 **Dates** (pitted)
2-3 Tbsps. **Chia**
3-4 Tbsps. **Water**
3 Tbsps. **Sesame tahini** (or hazelnut)

Instructions:

You can start by soaking the chia seeds in the water so it can gelatinize while we prepare the other ingredients.

Blend the flour with the cinnamon, the baking powder, and the nutmeg.

Next, puree the banana and blend with the coconut butter.

Add the fat mixture to the dry compounds and homogenize well.

Consecutively, add the grated ginger and stir again.

Now, combine the dates, the maples syrup, the tahini, and the soaked chia in a chopper and blend until fully homogeneous.

Next, transfer to the batter and stir and knead the cookie dough nicely.

You can use a robot to make the process easier.

Then, you can start heating the oven to 150° C - 160° C / 302° F - 320° F with a fan.

Now, you can roll out the dough between two sheets of parchment paper until you have a 5mm/0.2 inch layer.

If you do not wish to use the paper, just add more flour while rolling the dough to prevent it from sticking to the pin.

Cut the desserts in the desired shapes and sizes and arrange in a baking pan covered with parchment paper.

Bake for about 15 minutes until golden and leave them to cool down on a grid.

My notes:

No-bake Cinnamon Cookies with Blueberry Jam

Ingredients:

For the cookies:
1/2 cup **Oatmeal**
1/2 cup **Coconut shreds**
1/2 cup **Banana chips**
5-6 Tbsps. **Almond flour**
3-4 Tbsps. **Coconut sugar**
1 tsp. **Cinnamon**
3-4 Tbsps. **Coconut butter** (soft)

For the jam:
1 cup **Blueberries** (fresh or frozen)
1 Tbsp. **Apple pectin**
1 Tbsp. **Agave syrup** (or other sweetener of choice)
A few drops **Rose water** - optional

Instructions:

First, of course, we start with the cookies.

Place all ingredients (except the butter) in a kitchen chopper or a robot and homogenize the mixture.

Next, add the coconut butter and blend again.

Now, start forming the cookies by shaping them as small balls and pressing gently to make them flatter.

You can use cookie ring molds but it is not mandatory.

Arrange the desserts in a tray covered with parchment paper and transfer into the freezer for a few hours.

Meanwhile, we can continue with the jam.

It is ridiculously easy!

If the berries are frozen, first you have to leave them aside at room temperature to defrost.

Next, simply blend all ingredients until fully homogeneous.

When the cookies are ready, spread the blueberry jam on top and enjoy!

CANDIES, ENERGY BARS AND TRUFFLES

Fruit Jelly Candies

Ingredients:

2 **Bananas**
2 **Kiwis**
2 tsps. **Agar-agar**
2-3 Tbsps. **Water**
Some **Orange zest** (bio)
Some **Coconut shreds**

Instructions:

First, mix the agar and the water and stir to blend.

Next, puree the fruits and heat them in a metal pot on low temperature.

When the sweet mixture starts to simmer, add the agar and stir to homogenize the mass.

Add some grated orange zest to taste and stir again.

Let the cream simmer for a few minutes and take it off the heat.

Pour in a square container and leave it to cool down for several hours to gelatinize.

Cut in the desired shapes and cover with desiccated coconut.

Hazelnut Candies

Ingredients:

1/2 cup **Hazelnut tahini**
4 Tbsps. **Cocoa butter**
4 Tbsps. **Coconut butter**
6 Tbsps. **Honey** (or maple syrup for strict vegans)
3-4 Tbsps. **Cacao powder**
A fistful of **Hazelnuts**
A fistful of **Blueberries**

Instructions:

First, melt the cocoa and coconut butters in a double boiler on low temperature.

Remember not to let the water boil to avoid burning the butter.

Next, add the tahini, the honey, and the cacao powder.

Stir to blend the ingredients well.

Now, grind the hazelnuts and add them to the mixture along with the blueberries.

Stir to homogenize the mixture completely.

Take the sweet mass off the heat and pour it into your favorite candy molds.

Transfer the desserts into the freezer for several hours to set.

Raw Energy Candies

Ingredients:

1 cup **Dates** (pitted)
1/2 cup **Raw cashew**
2 Tbsps. **Coconut butter**
2 Tbsps. **Sesame tahini**
1 Tbsp. **Hazelnut tahini**

Instructions:

First, soak the cashews for at least 2 hours in some clean water.

Next, strain, and wash them thoroughly.

Now, we can continue preparing the candy dough.

Grind the dates in a kitchen chopper along with the cashew.

Next, add the remaining compounds and homogenize the mixture once again.

Bring the dough in the fridge for a few hours to set.

Finally, form the candies with whatever shapes and sizes you prefer.

If you wish, you can decorate with some coconut shreds, sesame seeds or cocoa powder.

Metabolism-boosting Chocolate Candies

Ingredients:

1/2 cup **Cocoa butter** (melted)
2 Tbsps. **Cacao powder**
2 Tbsps. **Honey** (or maple syrup for strict vegans)
2 Tbsps. **Coconut butter** (melted)
1 tsp. **Powdered chili peppers** (adjust to taste)

Instructions:

The preparation of these hot chocolate bites is very easy.

Simply combine all compounds in a kitchen chopper, a blender or a robot and homogenize the mixture completely.

Remember to add the chili powder slowly in order to control the hotness of the mixture.

If you do not tolerate too much of it, add a smaller amount.

Finally, pour the mixture into candy molds (or ice cube molds) and refrigerate for a few hours until they set.

Consume for up to two weeks, although I am sure they will disappear overnight!

No-bake Cookie Bites

Ingredients:

1 1/2 cup **Vegan cookies**
1/2 cup **Ground walnuts**
1/4 cup **Dry apricots**
4 Tbsps. **Coconut butter**
1/4 cup **Vegan chocolate*** (preferably sugar-free)
1/2 cup **Coconut cream**
1 Tbsp. **Water**
2 drops **Rum extract**
1/2 tsp. **Vanilla extract**

Instructions:

Crush the cookies and mince the apricots in small pieces. Next, mix them in a large bowl along with the walnuts and the vanilla.

Now, pour the cream in a metal pot and heat it on low temperature. Add the water, the coconut butter, the rum, and the chocolate and homogenize the mixture. Stir and blend until all the compounds are fully melted.

Next, transfer the liquid into the bowl and stir to blend with the dry ingredients. Divide the mixture into silicon muffin molds and place them in the freezer overnight to set. Remove from the molds and enjoy!

*If you do not have sugar-free chocolate, you can always make it on your own! You can find two of my favorite healthy chocolate recipes in my FREE ebook "12 Healthy Dessert Recipes"

Carrot Bites

Ingredients:

1 cup **Grated carrots**
1/2 cup **Ground walnuts**
5 **Dates** (pitted)
3/4 cup **Coconut butter** (melted)
2 Tbsps. **Desiccated coconut**
Some **Grated organic orange zest** - optional

Instructions:

Squeeze the juice from the carrots or you can recycle some carrot pulp from you vegetable juices.

Next, add the ground walnuts, the desiccated coconut and blend the compounds.

Now, puree the dates and add them to the mix along with the coconut butter.

Stir and blend the mixture well until fully homogeneous.

Form the bites with the desired sizes and cover with some grated orange zest, if you desire.

Arrange the desserts in a tray and transfer into the fridge for a few hours to set.

Enjoy!

Apricot Truffles

Ingredients:

1 1/2 cup **Raw cashew**
2/3 cup **Coconut shreds**
3-4 Tbsps. **Coconut butter** (soft)
Maple syrup – to taste
Some **Orange juice**
A fistful of **Dry apricots**
Some **Ground walnuts**

Instructions:

First, soak the cashew in some water for at least 4 hours.

Next, soak the apricots in the orange juice for about half an hour.

Use as much liquid as to fully cover the fruits.

Now, puree them along with the orange juice until homogenous.

Next, combine all ingredients (except the walnuts) in a kitchen chopper and blend completely.

Finally, form small balls and cover them with the ground nuts.

Bon appetite!

Avocado Truffles

Ingredients:

1 **Avocado**
20 **Dates** (pitted)
1/2 cup **Coconut butter** (soft)
1 Tbsp. **Carob powder**
3 Tbsps. **Cacao powder** (or cocoa)

Instructions:

The preparation of this recipe is ridiculously easy!

All you need to do is blend all the compounds in a kitchen chopper, a blender, or a robot until homogeneous.

Next, bring the mixture in the fridge for a few hours to harden a bit.

And finally, form the truffles as small balls and cover them with some cocoa (or cacao) powder.

Easy peasy!

My notes:

Cocoa Truffles

Ingredients:

1/2 cup **Raw cashew**
16 **Dates** (pitted)
1/2 cup **Wholegrain corn flakes**
7-8 Tbsps. **Cocoa beans**
3-4 Tbsps. **Carob powder**

Instructions:

The preparation is similar to the previous recipe.

Grind the cashew in a kitchen chopper or a robot.

Next, add the dates, half of the cocoa beans, the corn flakes, and blend again.

Now, scoop from the cocoa mass and form the truffles as small balls.

Finally, grind the rest of the cocoa beans and blend with the carob powder.

Cover the desserts with this mixture and place them in the fridge to set.

Voila!

Protein Truffles

Ingredients:

3-4 Tbsps. **Cocoa butter** (melted)
3-4 Tbsps. **Maple syrup**
2 Tbsps. **Cacao powder**
3-4 Tbsps. **Vegan protein powder***
1 tsp. **Cinnamon**

Instructions:

The preparation is very easy and simple.

Melt the cocoa butter in a double boiler, if not done so already.

Next, add the maple syrup, the protein, the cinnamon, and blend completely.

Finally, add the cacao and homogenize the mixture one last time.

Form the truffles and cover them with some more cacao powder.

Transfer into the fridge for a few hours to set.

* You can use any kind of plant-base protein – lupine, pea, pumpkin seed, sunflower, rice, etc. or a ready-made vanilla flavored blend of vegan protein powders.

Pumpkin Energy Truffles

Ingredients:

1 cup **Cooked pumpkin** (roasted, steamed, boiled)
1 cup **Ground almonds**
1 cup **Ground walnuts**
1 Tbsp. **Sesame tahini**
2 Tbsps. **Honey** (or maple syrup for strict vegans)
1 tsp. **Cinnamon**
3 1/2 Tbsps. **Desiccated coconut**
1 1/2 Tbsp. **Cacao powder**
1 Tbsp. **Coconut butter** (soft)

Instructions:

The preparation of this recipe follows the technology of most no-bake energy bites.

First, leave half a tablespoon of the desiccated coconut and the cacao powder for decorating the truffles.

Next, combine all compounds in a suitable kitchen appliance (a robot, a chopper or a blender) and homogenize the mixture.

Form the desserts with the desired shapes and sizes and cover with the coconut shreds and the cacao we saved from the first step.

Refrigerate for a few hours and enjoy!
So easy and so tasty!

Homemade Raffaello Candies

Ingredients:

2 cups **Dates** (pitted)
2 1/2 cups **Coconut shreds**
1/2 cup **Coconut cream**
3-4 Tbsps. (heaped) **Coconut butter** (soft)

Instructions:

First, grind the dates in a kitchen chopper or a robot.

Next, add the coconut cream, the butter, and 2 cups of the desiccated coconut.

Stir and blend the mixture nicely until fully homogeneous.

Transfer into the fridge for a few hours to set.

Finally, form the candies and cover them with the remaining coconut shreds.

Enjoy!

My notes:

Chestnut Bites

Ingredients:

1 cup **Edible chestnuts**
1/2 cup **Vegan chocolate*** (preferably sugar-free)
1/2 cup **Maple syrup**
1/2 cup **Ground almonds**
1 tsp. **Vanilla extract**
1 tsp. **Cinnamon**
A pinch of **Salt**
Ground nuts of choice

Instructions:

Peel the chestnuts and soak them in some water for at least 10-12 hours.

Next, strain, wash them with water, and boil with a pinch of salt until fully cooked.

Then, melt the chocolate in a double boiler and blend with the maple syrup, the vanilla and the cinnamon powder.

Now, you can strain the chestnuts and mince them in a kitchen chopper or a robot.

Next, combine all ingredients (except the ground nuts) and blend until fully homogenous. Finally, form small bites and cover them with the ground nuts (walnuts, almonds, pistachios, etc.)

*If you do not have sugar-free chocolate, you can always make it on your own! You can find two of my favorite healthy chocolate recipes in my FREE ebook "12 Healthy Dessert Recipes"

Raw Hemp Seed Bites

Ingredients:

1 Tbsp. **Chia seeds**
2 1/2 Tbsps. **Hemp seeds** (peeled)
1 **Banana**
1 1/2 Tbsp. **Tahini** (sesame, hazelnut, peanut)
1 Tbsp. **Coconut butter** (soft)
2 Tbsps. **Cacao powder**

Instructions:

First, mash the banana and mix it with the chia seeds. Wait for about 10 minutes for the chia to gelatinize the fruit.

Now, add 2 tablespoons of the hemp seeds, the tahini, the butter, and the cacao, and homogenize the mixture.

Transfer into a baking pan and press to form a thick flat layer.

Sprinkle the rest of the hemp sees on top and refrigerate for a few hours to set.

Cut in the desired shapes and sizes and the bites are ready for consumption!

My notes:

Fat Bombs (Low Carb)

Ingredients:

1/4 cup **Raw walnuts**
1/4 cup **Raw cashew**
5 tsps. **Cocoa butter** (melted)
1 Tbsp. **Coconut butter**
A fistful of **Berries** (blueberries, raspberries, blackberries, etc.)
3 tsps. **Desiccated coconut**

Instructions:

First, soak the cashew in some water for at least 2 hours.

Then, strain and wash them thoroughly.

Now, we can start preparing these delicious fat bombs!

Place the walnuts, the cocoa butter, and the desiccated coconut in a kitchen chopper (or a robot) and blend until homogeneous.

Next, divide the mixture into muffin molds and press gently to form the crusts of the desserts.

Consecutively, blend the cashew with the coconut butter, and the berries.

Pour the sweet cream on top of the first layer in the molds, and place the muffin tin in the freezer for about an hour to set.

Gluten-free Pumpkin Pancakes

Ingredients:

1 cup **Buckwheat flour**
1/2 cup **Pumpkin puree** (from roasted or steam pumpkin)
1/2 cup **Vegan milk**
3 Tbsps. **Coconut butter**
1 tsp. **Baking powder**
1/2 tsp. **Baking soda**
2 tsps. **Cinnamon**
1/4 tsp. **Nutmeg**
A pinch of **Salt**

Instructions:

The preparation of these yummy pancakes is ridiculously easy!

Simply blend all ingredients in a blender and homogenize the mixture until you reach the consistency of smooth and thick batter.

Cook the pastries in a hot skillet with some coconut butter as usual.

Garnish with whatever you prefer – maple syrup, seeds, sesame tahini, fruits, etc.

Find 300+ more gluten-free recipes for the whole family and for all occasions in "The Gluten Free Cookbook Series Bundle"!

Energy Bars – 3 Variations

Ingredients:

For the base "dough":
1 cup **Peanut butter**
1 cup **Coconut butter**
1 cup **Almond flour**
1 cup **Coconut flour**
1 cup **Oat bran** (or flax seed flour)
1 cup **Almond milk**

For variation 1:
2 Tbsps. **Peanut butter**
Some **Ground peanuts**

For variation 2:
1 Tbsp. **Matcha powder**
Some **Goji berries** (dry)

For variation 3:
Several **Dates to taste** (pitted)
Several **Dry apricots**
1 Tbsp. **Cocoa powder**
1 Tbsp. **Carob powder**
Stevia extract* – to taste
1 Tbsp. **Coconut butter**

Instructions:

First, we start preparing the base mixture for the energy bars.

Mix the peanut butter with the coconut butter and melt them in a double boiler.

Next, add the remaining ingredients for the "dough" and blend well. If you need to, adjust the quantities of the dry and liquid parts to reach the desired pliable consistency.

Divide the dough in three equal parts.

For the first variation, add the peanut butter to one part of the mixture and blend it nicely. Melt the peanut butter beforehand, if you wish to smoothen the process.

Next, roll out the dough at about 1 cm (0.4") and decorate with the ground peanuts. Place it in the freezer to set for several hours and cut it in the desired shapes.

For the second variation, take another part of the base mixture and mix it with the Matcha powder. Blend well and roll it out just like the first one.

Sprinkle some goji berries on top and put it in the freezer to keep its shape. Next, cut in the desired forms.

For the last variation, melt the coconut butter and place it in the blender. Add the remaining ingredients and blend well until you reach a homogenous paste.

Note: if the mixture becomes too dry and difficult to blend, add some water or milk.

Combine it with the base dough and mix well.

Finally, the last part is the same as the previous variations – roll the mixture out, and store in the freezer for a couple of hours. Next, cut in the desired shapes.

*The quantity of the stevia will depend on the type of product you use. Most extracts have a ratio to sugar as follows:

1 cup sugar = 1 tsp. liquid or powdered stevia

1 Tbsp. sugar = 1/4 tsp. powdered (6-9 drops liquid stevia)

1 tsp. sugar = a pinch of powdered (2-4 drops liquid stevia)

Keep in mind that there are other types of stevia extracts with different ratios, for example 1:1.

Eventually, experiment and see what quantities suit your taste best!

Oatmeal Energy Bars

Ingredients:

1 cup **Raw nuts of choice** (almonds, hazelnuts, walnuts, etc.)
1/2 cup **Fine oatmeal**
1 Tbsp. **Sesame seeds**
1 tsp. **Ground flax seeds**
3-4 Tbsps. **Carob powder**
1 cup **Dates** (pitted)
A fistful of **Raisins**
2 Tbsps. **Chia seeds**
3-4 Tbsps. **Honey** (or maple syrup for strict vegans)
Some **Water**

Instructions:

Start by soaking the dates and the raisins in two separate containers with some water for about half an hour.

Meanwhile, grind the nuts, the oatmeal, and the seeds.

Also, mix the chia seeds with some water for 15 minutes to gelatinize.

Now, we can continue assembling the batter for the energy bars.

Puree the dates and the raisins along with the water they were soaked in.

Next, mix all dry compounds – the ground nuts, oatmeal, seeds, and the carob powder.

Add the fruit purees from the dates and raisins, and add the honey.

Stir and homogenize the mixture completely.

If it seems too dry and difficult to blend, add some water to make the process easier.

Now, heat the oven to 180° C/ 356° F.

Next, take a flat baking pan and cover it with parchment paper.

Spread the mixture on top and press gently to flatten it.

Bake until golden and let the dessert cool down on a grid.

Cut in the desired shapes and sizes and enjoy!

Remember to store the energy bars in the fridge!

PUDDING AND CREAM RECIPES

Chocolate Chia Pudding

Ingredients:

1 1/2 cup **Nut milk of choice**
1/3 cup **Chia**
1/4 cup **Cocoa powder**
1/2 tsp. **Cinnamon**
1/4 tsp. **Salt** (sea or Himalayan)
10 **Dates** (pitted)

Instructions:

Simply place all ingredients in a blender and stir well.

When the mixture becomes fully homogenous, pour it in small dessert cups and place them in the fridge.

Cool the pudding for several hours or overnight to set. Enjoy!

My notes:

Protein Vanilla Chia Pudding

Ingredients:

1 1/2 cup **Nut milk of choice**
1/4 cup **Chia**
1 Tbsp. **Vegan protein*** (preferably vanilla flavored)
1 tsp. **Honey** (or maple syrup for strict vegans)
1 **Vanilla pod**
1/2 cup **Berries** (strawberries, raspberries, blueberries, etc.)

Instructions:

This chia pudding is extremely easy, but so nutritious and healthy!

Start by mixing the milk with the honey and stir until the sweetener dissolves completely.

Next, add the vanilla beans and the protein powder, and homogenize the mixture with a hand blender.

Now, mix the chia seeds with the vanilla milk and stir occasionally for the next 15 minutes.

Finally, transfer the pudding into the fridge and leave it to gelatinize for several hours or overnight.

Decorate with some berries before serving!

* You can use any kind of plant-base protein – pea, pumpkin seed, sunflower, rice, etc. or a ready-made vanilla flavored blend of vegan protein powders.

Fruit Pudding

Ingredients:

1 **Pear** (fully ripe)
1 **Banana**
1 **Orange**
1/2 cup **Water**
2 Tbsps. **Corn starch** (non-GMO)

Instructions:

Remove the seeds from the pear and puree it in a blender or a kitchen chopper.

Add the banana and blend the fruits.

Next, squeeze the juice from the citrus and add it to the mixture along with the water.

Homogenize the mixture one more time and transfer into a metal pot.

Heat the smoothie on low temperature.

Meanwhile, mix the corn starch with a few tablespoons of water and add it to the mixture.

Stir and cook the pudding until you reach the desired consistency.

Melon&Raspberry Ice Pudding

Ingredients:

For the base:
Several **Dry pineapple slices**

For the pudding:
1 cup **Creamed coconut**
1 cup **Almond cream**
4-5 Tbsps. **Cocoa butter** (melted)
1 Tbsp. **Hibiscus powder**
3 Tbsps. **Agave syrup**
1 cup **Raspberries**
1 cup **Melon**

Instructions:

This recipe is ridiculously easy but extremely tasty!

Place the creamed coconut and the almond cream in a blender and homogenize the compounds.

Next, add the remaining ingredients for the cream (except the cocoa butter).

Blend again until fully homogeneous.

Now, add the butter and switch on the blender one more time.

Pour the cream in a muffin tin and put a dry pineapple slice on top of each cup.

Place the desserts in the freezer until they harden.

Finally, release and decorate with whatever you wish!

Hazelnut Banana Cream

Ingredients:

4 **Bananas**
1/2 **Pear**
3 Tbsps. **Hazelnut tahini**
3-4 Tbsps. **Coconut butter** (soft)

Instructions:

As usual, just blend the ingredients in a blender or a kitchen chopper and the cream is ready!

Pour into dessert cups and refrigerate for a few hours. That's it!

My notes:

Homemade Hazelnut Spread

Ingredients:

1 cup **Raw hazelnuts**
1 tsp. **Coconut butter** (soft)
1 tsp. **Cacao powder**
1 tsp. **Honey** (or maple syrup for strict vegans)
Coconut milk

Instructions:

First, soak the hazelnuts overnight with some clean water.

Next, strain, wash them thoroughly and bake in the oven at low temperature until they can be easily peeled.

Remove the hazelnuts' skins and grind the nuts in a kitchen chopper.

Now, add the butter, the cacao, and the honey, and blend completely.

Finally, start adding the coconut milk as you continue to blend the mixture.

Add as much liquid as you wish to reach the desired consistency.

Voila!

Very Simple Cacao Cream

Ingredients:

1 1/2 cup **Coconut milk**
3/4 cup **Coconut butter**
A fistful of **Dates** (pitted)
1-2 Tbsps. **Cacao powder**

Instructions:

The recipe is very simple and easy!

You just need to blend the compounds until homogeneous.

Adjust the quantities of the dates and the cacao to match your preferred taste.

Pour the cream into dessert cups and refrigerate for a few hours to set.

Voila!

My notes:

Chocolate Parfait

Ingredients:

2 cups **Raw cashew**
1 1/2 cup **Water** (filtered or spring)
2 Tbsps. **Lemon juice** (freshly squeezed)
3 Tbsps. **Honey** (or maple syrup for strict vegans)
1 **Vanilla pod**
2 Tbsps. **Cacao powder**
5-6 **Mint sprigs** (fresh)

Instructions:

Start by soaking the cashew nuts in some water for at least 4 hours or overnight.

Next, strain and wash them thoroughly.

Place the nuts in a blender and add the filtered water, the lemon juice, the vanilla beans, and the honey.

Stir to homogenize the mixture completely.

Now, transfer half of the cream into a clean container – we will need it later on.

Next, add the mint to the cream in the kitchen appliance and blend completely.

Divide the cream into dessert cups.

Now, bring back the other half of the cashew mixture in the blender and add the cacao powder.

Homogenize the mixture as well. If the taste seems too bitter, add more of the sweetener.

Pour the chocolate cream on top of the mint one, and bring the desserts in the fridge for several hours to set.

Voila!

Mint Ice Cream

Ingredients:

2 **Bananas**
1 1/2 cup **Raw cashew**
Some **Fresh mint leaves** (to taste)
3 Tbsps. **Cacao powder**
1 Tbsp. **Honey** (or maple syrup for strict vegans)

Instructions:

First, soak the cashew in some clean water for at least 2 hours.

Next, peel the bananas and cut them in slices.

Now, strain the nuts and wash then thoroughly with water.

Place them in a blender along with the banana slices, the mint leaves, and the honey.

Homogenize the mixture well, and add the cacao powder.

Stir one last time and the ice cream is ready for the final step.

Pour the mixture into suitable molds and freeze overnight.

Chocolate Mousse with Ginger

Ingredients:

2 cups **Raw sunflower seeds**
1/2 cup **Raw almonds**
1 cup **Raisins**
2 Tbsps. **Flax seeds**
2 Tbsps. **Coconut butter**
1 average **Ginger root** (adjust to taste)
2 Tbsps. **Cacao powder**
1 Tbsp. **Cinnamon**

Instructions:

First, separately soak the sunflower seeds, the flax seeds, and the almonds in some clean water for several hours.

Next, strain, wash them thoroughly with clean water and blend them in a kitchen chopper until homogeneous.

Transfer the mixture into a large cup or a bowl.

Next, blend the ginger root with the remaining ingredients. Add some water, if you need to make the process easier. Remember that ginger has a rather strong taste and flavor, so adjust the quantity according to your preferences.

Now, combine both mixture and blend until fully homogeneous.

Divide into dessert cups and enjoy!

Chocolate Mousse with Aquafaba

Ingredients:

3/4 cup **Chickpea aquafaba***
1/2 cup **Vegan chocolate** (preferably sugar-free)**
2-3 tsps. **Vanilla extract**

Instructions:

First, whisk the chickpea stock until stiff. Use a hand mixer or a blender to make the process easier.

Next, melt the chocolate in a double boiler on low heat and blend it with the vanilla.

Now, gently combine both compounds and stir carefully with a spatula.

Divide into suitable dessert cups and store in the fridge.

*Aquafaba is the vegetable stock left from boiling legumes such as beans, lentils, chickpeas, etc.

When preparing this vegan ingredient, it is best to throw away the "first water" from the cooked beans and use the second batch of vegetable stock.

*If you do not have sugar-free chocolate at your disposal, you can always make it on your own! You can find two of my favorite healthy chocolate recipes in my FREE ebook "12 Healthy Dessert Recipes"

Homemade Chocolate Cream

Ingredients:

1 **Banana**
1/2 **Avocado**
1 tsp. **Cacao powder**
1 tsp. (heaped) **Hazelnut tahini**
Maple syrup (agave) – to taste

Instructions:

This is a fool-proof easy recipe for a homemade chocolate cream that can be prepared in a minute!

Simply combine all ingredients in a kitchen chopper or a robot and blend until homogeneous.

That's it!

Pineapple Cream with Muesli

Ingredients:

1 cup **Silkened tofu**
1 cup **Vegan milk** (flavored)
1/2 cup **Oatmeal** (or sugar-free muesli)
1/4 cup **Raisins**
3 Tbsps. **Maple syrup**
1/2 **Pineapple**

Instructions:

This is a very simple and very delicious dessert recipe – excellent for breakfast or an afternoon snack!

First, peel the pineapple and cut the fruit in pieces.

Puree it in a blender along with the maple syrup.

Next, add the tofu and the vegan milk, and blend again.

Combine the pineapple cream with the muesli and the raisins in a bowl, and stir to homogenize the mixture.

Divide into dessert cups and serve! Mmmmmm!

Coconut Porridge (Low Carb)

Ingredients:

4 Tbsps. **Coconut shreds** (full-fat)
10 Tbsps. **Coconut milk**
1 Tbsp. **Coconut flour**
10-12 Tbsps. **Water**
Some **Vanilla extract**
A fistful of **Berries** - optional

Instructions:

First, heat the water on low temperature. Next, add the coconut shreds and half of the coconut milk and let it simmer for a minute.

Now, add the vanilla extract and the coconut flour. Stir to homogenize the mixture - add more water if it's too thick and dry. Finally, take the dessert off the heat, add the remaining of the milk, and garnish with the fruits!

Raspberry Panna Cotta

Ingredients:

2 cups **Vegan cream** (20% fat)
1/2 cup **Nut milk of choice**
4 tsps. **Agar-agar**
Some **Water** – for the agar
Maple syrup – to taste
1 cup **Raspberries**

Instructions:

Cover the agar with some water and wait for it to melt.

In the meantime, take half of the raspberries and 1 tablespoon of the maple syrup and heat them on low temperature.

Blend them with a hand blender and let the fruits simmer for a bit.

Next, strain the sweet syrup from the seeds and leave it aside to cool down.

Meanwhile, mix the cooking cream, the milk, and the remaining maple syrup in a metal pot, and heat them as well. When the vegan dairy products blend completely, take them off the heat.

Next, add a little bit more water to the agar and heat it in a double boiler.

Stir until it melts completely.

Now, take 2 tablespoons of the agar and mix it with the raspberry syrup.

Blend the remaining of it (the agar-agar) with the vegan dairy mixture.

Finally, is it time to assemble the panna cottas.

Take some dessert cups (or muffin molds) and place 1-2 tablespoons of the raspberry syrup in each one of them.

Place them in the freezer for several minutes for the raspberry jelly to stiffen.

Now, fill the cups with the cream and place them in the fridge for the agar-agar to do its magic!

Bon Appetite!

Very Simple Citrus Panna Cotta

Ingredients:

1/2 cup **Coconut milk**
1/2 cup **Orange juice**
1 Tbsp. **Maple syrup** (or coconut sugar, stevia*, etc.)
2 Tbsps. **Agar-agar**

Instructions:

Mix the coconut milk with the orange juice, and the maple syrup in a metal pot.

Heat the mixture above body temperature and stir until the sweetener is fully melted and blended.

Mix the agar with some water and stir until it melts.

Next, add it to the main mixture and blend to fully homogenize the compounds.

Pour into muffin molds or dessert cups and refrigerate for several hours until the panna cottas are fully set.

Release from the molds, garnish with some jam or jelly and enjoy!

*The quantity of the stevia will depend on the type of product you use. Most extracts have a ratio to sugar as follows:

1 cup sugar = 1 tsp. liquid or powdered stevia

1 Tbsp. sugar = 1/4 tsp. powdered (6-9 drops liquid stevia)

1 tsp. sugar = a pinch of powdered (2-4 drops liquid stevia)

Keep in mind that there are other types of stevia extracts with different ratios, for example 1:1.

Eventually, experiment and see what quantities suit your taste best!

My notes:

Sweet Rice Semolina Meal

Ingredients:

1/2 cup **Rice semolina**
2 cups **Nut milk of choice**
2 Tbsps. **Coconut butter**
Some **Sweetener of choice** (maple syrup, agave, stevia*, etc.) – to taste
Some **Cinnamon** – for decoration

Instructions:

First, start melting the butter in a metal pot on low temperature.

Next, add the semolina, stir well, and wait for it to absorb all of the butter.

Consecutively, slowly and gently start adding the milk in a thin stream while continue stirring the mixture.

Finally, add the sweetener and blend the batter until it reaches the desired consistency.

Now, take a dessert cup (or cups) and moist them on the inside. Pour the semolina meal and wait for it to cool down completely.

Turn the cup upside down to release the dessert and sprinkle some cinnamon at the top.

That's it! Easy-peasy!

*The quantity of the stevia will depend on the type of product you use. Most extracts have a ratio to sugar as follows:

1 cup sugar = 1 tsp. liquid or powdered stevia

1 Tbsp. sugar = 1/4 tsp. powdered (6-9 drops liquid stevia)

1 tsp. sugar = a pinch of powdered (2-4 drops liquid stevia)

Keep in mind that there are other types of stevia extracts with different ratios, for example 1:1.

Eventually, experiment and see what quantities suit your taste best!

Thank you!

I want to thank you for purchasing this book and reading it all the way to the end. I hope it has been helpful and informative. If you liked this volume, you can support my work and make it more visible for others who are looking for this kind of knowledge! I would deeply appreciate if you take a minute and write a short review on Amazon. I thank you in advance for your support!
Kind regards and best wishes,
Milica

P.S. And don't forget to get your free ebooks:
"10 Powerful Immune Boosting Recipes"
"12 Healthy Dessert Recipes"
"15 Delicious & Healthy Smoothies"
"The Complete Ayurveda Detox"

Go to *www.MindBodyAndSpiritWellbeing.com* and claim your gifts!

Or simply scan the QR code below:

About the author

Milica Vladova dedicated her work to spread the valuable knowledge of the physical, emotional, and spiritual wellbeing. She is determined to make the world healthier, happier, and more successful!

Her works have been published on **Dr. Axe, The Huffington Post**, **Thrive Global**, **The Elephant Journal**, **Sivana Spirit**, **YogiApproved**, **Steven Aitchison**, and more.

Find her on:
http://mindbodyandspiritwellbeing.com
https://facebook.com/**mindbodyandspiritwellbeing**
https://www.pinterest.com/**milicavladova**
https://twitter.com/**Holistic_Milky**

Milica is also the author of:

The Healthy Vegan Recipes Cookbook

MORE THAN 80 HEALTHY VEGAN RECIPES FOR THE WHOLE FAMILY!

In this volume you will find:
- Healthy vegan **main course dishes**;
- **Bread and salty snacks** recipes.
- **Dips and side dishes**.
- Yummy **sugar-free desserts**.
- Interesting info about **the numerous benefits of vegan foods**. and more!

★★★★★Perfect when you're in a pinch!

    I referred to this recipe book several times over the past week to get some healthy, tasty recipes for my vegan/vegetarian friends. The author definitely has first-hand experience preparing these dishes, provides clear tips and alternatives, and also imparts knowledge about the health benefits. I'm short, it's a practical recipe book, but it's also an insightful read. I'll be reaching for this book over the holiday season for more inspiration. I'm thinking of pulling together a raw nut loaf and I'm pretty sure I saw a recipe in here I could swing! I know it won't disappoint! (I'm considering purchasing a hard copy this Xmas for a raw food friend!)

    ~ Cynthia Luna on Amazon.com

★★★★★Try these recipes!

    Lots of wonderful recipes that I cannot wait to try. Healthy and nutritious meals! Snacks!

    ~ Aisha Hashmi on Amazon.com

The Gluten Free Cookbook Series Bundle

300+ YUMMY GLUTEN-FREE RECIPES FOR ALL OCCASIONS!

"The Gluten Free Cookbook Series Bundle" is your ultimate wheat-free cooking bible!
You can find everything from tasty snacks, side dishes and dips, to delicious main course meals and desserts!

This book bundle is comprised of:
> Part I: "Easy Gluten Free Desserts"
> Part II: "Gluten Free Cooking"
> Part III: "More Gluten Free Recipes"

What are you going to find in this bundle?

A ton of healthy recipes, low carb, and vegan ideas for the whole family:

=> **Healthy pancakes** packed with fiber;
=> **Delicious cakes** and pies with healthy sugar alternatives;
=> Gluten-free **muffins, brownies, and cookies**;
=> Wheat-free **bread and bun recipes**;
=> Gluten-free **pizza ideas**;
=> Delicious **Keto snacks**;
=> **Vegan meals** and side dishes;
=> **Heartwarming soups**;
=> and so much more!

You are going to have everything you need to jump-start your gluten-free journey!

Start healing your gut transforming your life TODAY with "The Gluten Free Cookbook Series Bundle"!

★★★★★I am very pleased with the Gluten Free cookbook as it contains recipes!

I am very pleased with the Gluten Free cookbook as it contains recipes from different parts of the world, both sweet and savoury.

I have tried some of the desserts and savoury dishes plus the bread and buns, and I must say I was very pleased with the taste and the results.

I am one of the individuals who have an allergy to wheat and all products with a gluten content. I am always looking for new gluten free recipes.

The Author has written a wonderful book with good explanation and recipes. Highly recommended.

~ Stella C. on Amazon.com

Complete Body Cleansing and Strong Immunity Bundle

- **Healthy recipes** with white sugar and white flour alternatives!
- Plenty of toning, refreshing, and cleansing **smoothie recipes!**
- Detoxing and strengthening aromatic **herbal blends!**
- Loads of delicious **immune boosting recipes** and remedies.
- Which exercises can help us **expel more toxins** from our cells;
- **Simple weekly, monthly, and annual detox rituals** to help you boost your energy, lose weight naturally, fight chronic fatigue, and prevent from diseases.
- How to purify your system **without starving**?
- How to **deeply detox and heal your colon, liver, kidneys, lungs, lymph**, and more?
- How to naturally **get rid of parasites**?
- **Healthy gut - healthy you!** How to take care of our beneficial colon bacteria?
- **Natural probiotics and prebiotics** - how to make them at home with natural ingredients?
- **Adaptogens** - the key to dealing with stress, infertility and building our strong immunity.
- Natural ways and systems to **prevent, stop, and heal from cancer** cell formation.
- **The best herbs, essential oils and homeopathic remedies** to prevent from diseases, viruses, fungi, and bacteria.
- and much more!

★★★★★Science mixed with love for a winning combo

What a wealth of information filled with knowledge and innate insight into how the body functions and heals. So many great choices offered. These books are wonderful at dipping into every day for fresh ideas. Just applying some of the knowledge is still so powerful at helping you get fit and healthy from the inside out. Great recipes and full of science mixed with genuine love from the author.

~ **Reviewer on Amazon.com**

★★★★★Accessible, clear, and gently written

I wish all health books were written this way!

First, Ms. Vladova shares exhaustive information on cleansing and eating well with such a gentle, non-judgemental attitude.

And she meets the reader where they are. For instance, after introducing the Weekly Fasting Day with just tea or Water, Ms. Vladova suggest that if that is too extreme for you at the beginning, you can start with a day of fasting that involves Green Smoothies instead. And if even that is too much, she offers a plan for a day with just rice and apples.

As someone who's never tried any cleanses, her approach was so accessible!

Second, there is NO FLUFF! She gets right into talking about how to eat better and cleanse your body.

Recipes are easy to understand and well explained.

~ **J D on Amazon.com**

★★★★★ **The Perfect Christmas Stocking Filler - A Recovery Programme for those who Overindulge**

Gosh, this is a must-buy for anyone who cares about their body.

I'd already had some great results from the Healthy Body Cleanse detox programme, but the other two books are an absolute bargain - so full of useful information to keep you on track.

Although it's a great Christmas pressie for those of us who have no willpower in the season of gross overindulgence, it's actually a great regime to follow in the month before to prepare your body for the onslaught.

A win-win either way.

~ FireDancer on Amazon.com

★★★★★**A great resource!**

What a wonderful resource, so jam-packed with information! The body has a great mechanism to heal itself and these books help with that. I'm really pleased because my daily smoothies are now more interesting with the recipes included. The other recipes are easily adapted if you are vegan like I am. This bundle is what I would term a coffee-table book because once you've read it through you can dip into it every day or whenever you need to be reminded of the great info inside. My health has greatly improved and I recommend this bundle to anyone on the same journey to health or thinking about it.

~ Karen Aminadra on Amazon.com

DIY Homemade Beauty Products Bundle

MORE THAN 500 NATURAL ORGANIC BEAUTY RECIPES FOR THE WHOLE BODY!

What are you going to find in this book?
- Universal **face masks** for all skin types.
- **Lotions and cremes** for oily, dry, and mature skin.
- **Anti-aging and rejuvenating serums** for the face and eye contour.
- Natural **remedies for acne, pimples, blackheads**, etc.
- Gentle **whitening treatments** for brighter complexion and radiant skin.
- Universal nourishing **hair masks**;
- **Hair repair** recipes;
- **Anti-split ends** treatments;
- Natural **remedies for hair-loss** and thinning hair;
- **Hair growth** stimulators;
- **Dandruff healing masks** and ointments for oily and itchy scalp;
- **Herbal rinsing, organic shampoo recipes** and oil blends;
- Nourishing **body butters and lotions**;
- **Non-toxic sunscreen** recipes;
- Cleansing and healing **body scrubs and exfoliators**;
- **Anti-cellulite treatments** and massaging oils;
- Nourishing and **anti-aging hand cremes** and masks;
- **Nail strengthening** procedures;
- Natural **toothpastes and mouthwashes**;
- and more...

★★★★★Great deal!

This budle is a great resource for homemade beauty products! These are gentle and natural products!

~ Kelly Phister on Amazon.com

★★★★★Great set of books that has numerous recipes for everyone

Great set of books that has numerous recipes for every item.

The ingredients required are not difficult to come by. Overall a very nice and helpful set of books that comes in very handy for lotions and hand creams, hair masks etc. I recommend this book.

~ Joanne Beal on Amazon.com

★★★★★Start saving money and be healthier, too!

Talk about your natural resource for all things you purchase. Now I am the first one to tell people to stop buying prepare items like soap, shampoo and the like, and to make their own. I go to Lush religiously and purchase their items. It is all natural barring a few essential ingredients that are needed to preserve the products, and even them it is as gentle and natural as possible. Show yourself some love and get this book, and save yourself some money at Lush, because their products are not cheap and this DIY boom is loaded with so much and really is worth the small price investment as you will save literally thousands with all these recipes and all the imformation!

~ Aisha Hashmi on Amazon.com

Printed in Great Britain
by Amazon